How Do We Get There?

How Do We Get There?

A Critique of the Question 'What Do You Do?'

James Herod

New York City
1973

How Do We Get There?
A Critique of the Question 'What Do You Do?'

© 2018 by James Herod

Published by the Lantern Library
https://thelanternlibrary.wordpress.com

Written in 1973
First published as a printed book in 2018

ISBN: **978-0-9983797-1-5**

Type set in SchoolBook
5" x 8," 128 pages

Book and Cover design by
Rosalie Montenigro

Cover image of maze licensed from:
mazegenerator.net

More of the author's work can be found at:
www.jamesherod.info

Contents

Prefatory Note 7

Explanations for Acronyms Used 11

1 Preliminaries...................................13

2 Why is the Question 'What Do You Do?' a
Vanguard Question 29

3 The Proletariat and Protagonists of
the Proletariat....................................49

4 If it is Dogmatic to Fight to Build a
Vanguard Party Why Isn't It Just as
Dogmatic to Fight to Establish a Network
of Councils? 61

5 How Do We Agitate for the
Proletariat's Emancipation of Itself? 79

Prefatory Note
April 2007

(1) In my *Draft Constitution* of November 1970 I arrived at a definition of communism which formed the backdrop of all my writings of the 1970s. I thought of a free society as "a network of workers councils united on the basis of direct democracy." Somewhere along the way I shifted away from a strict focus on the workplace (that is, away from a strict anarcho-syndicalist orientation) and adopted a three-pronged approach involving neighborhood assemblies, workplace assemblies, and (extended) household assemblies. This new focus got written up in my book *Getting Free*. Fortunately, because the principle of direct democracy was so central for me, most of the reasoning in this book from 1973 is more or less relevant also to the task of establishing "an association of democratic autonomous neighborhoods."

(2) I'm no longer an advocate of armed

struggle, however. I just don't think it can work, and its costs are too high.

(3) In a few passages in this book I had unwittingly passed on the Marxist misuse of the word anarchism as a term for fanatic individualism. I've edited those out, and substituted the terms individualism, fanatic individualism, or egoism, which is what I was actually talking about. The meaning was not affected at all. I think this is fair and warranted. There is no sense perpetuating the century-old Marxist disparagement of anarchism and needlessly alienating contemporary revolutionaries, most of whom are anarchists.

(4) By "proletarian" I meant practically everyone, since I believe most people in the United States are in the working class (minus 30-40 million petty bourgeois and 5-10 million ruling class people). So I was actually writing about "majoritarian" issues. I eventually stopped using the term, however. It's too loaded. But you should not let its usage here prevent you from understanding this book. I was not using it to refer to the much more limited "industrial working class."

(5) By "third road" I meant neither Bolshevism nor Social Democracy, neither Lenin nor Kautsky – not what later in the 1980s came to be called the Third Road in European politics, namely, a kind of reformist communism.

Addendum (2018)

Well, it is certainly embarrassing to me today to read in this book that I quoted Marx's criticism of Bakunin. In 1973 I didn't know much about Bakunin, although I had read some Kropotkin and had explored Colin Ward's *Anarchy* magazine. But I came into the left mostly via the council communism of Anton Pannekoek. It was not until a decade or so later that I abandoned a strict, orthodox focus on workers' councils in favor of the more classical anarcho-communism.

It has been obvious for quite a few decades now that Marx's insistence that the state could be used to get rid of the state was terribly mistaken, and that Bakunin's argument that we needed to bypass the state in getting to communism was the correct strategy. This disagreement, which led to the split in the First International, and the resultant hegemony of Marxism in the anti-capitalist movement to this very day, was an enormous tragedy to befall leftist revolutionaries. This historical wrong turn has by now been thoroughly researched, most particularly in two recent books: Robert Graham, *We Do Not Fear Anarchy, We Invoke It: The First International and the Origin of the Anarchist Movement* (2015), and Wolfgang Eckhardt, *The First Socialist Schism: Bakunin vs. Marx in the Internation-*

al Workingmen's Association (2016).

But in this book I was focusing on Marx's more democratic views, namely, that only the working class could free itself, and that communism meant the free association of the direct producers. So my deliberations on an egalitarian strategy for liberation are still relevant, I hope.

By the way, I long ago stopped using the phrase Marxist-Leninist. It is practically a crime to link Marx with Lenin. Lenin was a much inferior thinker, and his Bolshevik revolution was a blow to the anti-capitalist struggle from which we have still not fully recovered. In fact, it may have derailed what was probably our best chance to get free from capitalism. Will we ever get another one?

Explanations for Acronyms Used

NLR = New Left Review;
YAWF = Youth Against War and Fascism;
SWP = Socialist Workers Party;
IWA = International Workingmen's
   Association;
SDS = Students for a Democratic Society;
RYMII = Revolutionary Youth Movement II;
CRV = Committee of Returned Volunteers;
Mobe = New Mobilization Against the War;
OL = October League;
RU = Revolutionary Union;
PL = Progressive Labor;
CP = Communist Party.

Chapter One
Preliminaries

I want to try to set down on paper a critique of the question `What do you do?' This is the question that is invariably asked whenever anyone raises the issue of egalitarian politics. Even though I have a small stack of working papers on this problem already I am rarely able in my personal conversations to get into any of these issues, even when the question What do you do? is genuinely put, and is not used as simply a bludgeon to halt any serious discussion of an egalitarian conception of the revolution (as it often is). Perhaps I am going about it backwards, but I never seem to get beyond certain preliminary remarks:

(1) The question is itself a vanguard question.

(2) Almost no thought or effort has gone into figuring out how to establish a `network

of workers councils united on the basis of direct democracy`, which is the phrase I use to describe my conception of socialist democracy, and so it probably seems to be a lot more vague and difficult than it actually is (at least this is a possibility).

(3) The question is often merely a dodge, a way to avoid having to consider the nonvanguard approach or avoid having to abandon, at least momentarily for the purposes of discussion, the vanguard image. That is, the question sometimes reflects an entrenched unwillingness to even consider seriously an egalitarian strategy because of a prior, if only implicit, commitment to vanguard politics.

(4) The egalitarian, collective image of the revolution is so thoroughly absent from current trends and traditions (which tend to coalesce around either an individualist or vanguardist image) that people tend to respond to the network of councils proposal with disbelief. They say things like ``I don't see any other way'' (than the vanguard approach) – a position that is very often rooted in other beliefs, which can be discovered by digging around a bit: in a belief for example that an egalitarian society is impossible because all societies are necessarily stratified (i.e., ``there will always be leaders''). Or they may say that the egalitarian conception of the revolution is utopian, a position which, it usually turns out, is rooted in a fixed conception of human nature and a

dualistic conception of knowledge. Sometimes they simply reject the idea of an egalitarian strategy as preposterous.

But even when the question is genuinely put and reflects a real interest in council communism I can't seem to get into the concrete details of the answer. Maybe I don't have an answer, or at least not a firm one. But I don't think this is the case anymore. I don't even think it was true during the splits of recent years. I could have said lots of concrete things about the strategy of winning a network of workers councils but the atmosphere was so hostile to any rational discussion it was impossible to sit down and work the issue through. I think that is what happened. My opponents in these arguments were unwilling to adopt, as a problem to be solved, the working out of the strategy implicit in the council idea. They were after fast and ready solutions, something that could be easily comprehended and written up so that they could ``get on with the job.'' They were not interested in taking the network of councils idea over as a goal and then sitting down with others to hash out the means to get there. I think that's why I resisted giving concrete answers to the question. And the times I did attempt it I got shouted down before I could finish two sentences.

Vanguardists put means ahead of ends. They come at it backwards.[1] I ask first: what is com-

1 Lukacs said that Stalinism is when we put prac-

munism? And then: how do we get there? They look first to what seems to be possible (organizing a party, for example) and then settle for where organizing will get you, to the party's seizure of power. I don't think in these terms at all, and consequently I find it necessary first of all to challenge the very framework of the discussion. Unfortunately, discussion never seems to get beyond this. The question `What do you do?' when posed by vanguardists is always a loaded one. They expect you to sit there and spell out a set of practical steps you can take, things you can *do*, steps you can be sure will then be ridiculed as absurd and preposterous, which they undoubtedly do appear to those for whom the overall goal, content, and nature of the revolution is apparently off limits to discussion.

I want to return to some of these preliminary considerations in a minute, particularly to the

tice first, ahead of theory. He said Stalinists don't have a theory, but act out of the expediency of power politics. Is this true? I'm not so sure this is true. Such an opinion seems to me to be based on the very duality it is trying to avoid. Vanguardists do have a goal, but they are two-faced about it. Their stated goal is to seize (or keep) power, which they present as the proletariat's seizure of power. Their practice doesn't jive with their stated goal. Perhaps that's why Lukacs was led to say they place practice first. But it does jive very well with their real goal, their implicit goal – the party's seizure of power and the establishment of a new bourgeois tyranny. Obviously, all vanguardists deny that they are attempting to seize power for themselves. I hope to show further on why we should not take them at their own word.

idea that the very question is itself a vanguard question. They is a key insight, I am convinced, and must be developed. In any case, the question `What do you do?' is certainly a natural one and comes easily for most of us. But it is one, I believe, that flows naturally and spontaneously only out of the dualistic framework that most of us have spent our lives trapped inside of. Before proceeding further however it might help to try to reconstruct briefly my own history of trying to come to grips with this question.

I don't think there has ever been a time since 1968 when the question of strategy hasn't been there. During the Columbia strike there were long debates about strategy, but these were not so much arguments about strategy for revolution in the whole society as they were debates about strike strategy and related issues. Moreover, in spite of these strategy discussions, the biggest question for me during the Columbia strike was not so much about strategy as about what constitutes a Just Authority? The riddle for me was: if the strike is justified because the present set up is indefensible, then what arrangement of things would be defensible? This was merely a reflection of my larger interest in the just society, as I then phrased it. It is certainly without question also that throughout the academic year 1968-1969, when I taught at Pratt and Hunter, the main theoretical puzzle for me concerned the structure of the democratic society, since the strike had convinced me that contemporary U.S. society is a ruling class society, and since I was convinced also that Russia likewise was not a democratic or socialist society.

I was working with the idea of workers councils at that time because of the lectures I had heard Ernest Mandel give in the fall of 1968 and because of my own digging around in the journals. I also had the idea of direct democracy because of Robert Paul Wolff's lectures and his mimeographed essay on political theory, which I read in the summer or fall of 1968 (later published as *In Defense of Anarchism*). I remember arguing the concept of direct democracy at Pratt and Hunter from every possible angle for nine solid months, with almost no one defending it except me. Nevertheless, I felt that none of the assaults on the idea all year were successful. Wolff's essay played a big role that year. I put his critique of democratic theory on the board dozens of times. And I would always end by saying: so we don't have a theory of democracy. I never accepted Wolff's own conclusion, and I know that simultaneously with this acceptance of Wolff's demonstration that traditional theories of democracy don't hang together I was arguing in other lectures against (what I later saw as) the central assumption of his critique – the autonomy of the individual. The idea of overcoming individualism was one of the main elements in my stress on councils.

At any rate, it was not until sometime in 1970 that I worked out of Wolff's trap and transcended the impasse he had got himself into, in a short critique of his position and of his presupposed ethic of individual autonomy as the supreme value.[2] Once this insight had been reached everything took on a new light.

By the end of the term in the spring of 1969 the basic image of the just society that I now have had been worked out. This was further

2 The problem with Wolff's critique is that he does not take into account the sociological (this should read social, that is, Marx's, since he was the first to advance a genuinely social point of view) critique of the Kantian theory of the moral autonomy of the individual. Rather, he accepts the Kantian view. He bases his critique of classical democratic theory upon it, and thus concludes, rightly, that since both the majority vote and representatives violate individual autonomy that democratic theory is a failure. He concludes that anarchism (seen as an aggregate of autonomous individuals) is the only thing left, and that there is no legitimate authority.

The real problem with classical democratic theory is that first of all it was never in fact applied. Rather the ruling class has controlled society. And secondly, it was formulated in terms of an individualistic ethic and based on the so-called autonomy of the individual. Wolff's critique inadvertently shows both the weakness of classical theory and the limitations of Wolff. Macpherson's critique is equally cogent, but he also refuses to draw the necessary conclusions. Neither does Rawls.

The trouble with radical democratic theory however is that it appears to be only more or less the same theory but without the ruling class. I feel that the real essence of the Marxian view of democracy has never been explicitly stated, never explicated, and the idea of collective leadership never clearly spelled out." (From notes of June 16, 1970 entitled `The Meaning of Collective Leadership.')

formalized in December of that year in a one page `Model of a Just Society' for a seminar I was giving for the Committee of Returned Volunteers. It was written up in response to a very clear impasse that had been reached in the seminar the week before over what the democratic society would look like. Then a year later the whole thing jelled out in the still more concrete form of a draft constitution.

What I am trying to get at here I guess is whether or to what extent the questions of goal and strategy have been separate for me like I have sometimes tended to think. It is true that for a first period after moving into the radical movement I focused more on the problem of the goal (up to the draft constitution of November 1970), and then for a second period focused more on the question of strategy, particularly on a critique of the vanguard strategy. Nevertheless, the two things have been intertwined all along. I know for example that in response to one of the main arguments against direct democracy from students at Pratt and Hunter in 1968-1969, namely that the majority of people didn't have the knowhow to vote on issues of basic policy and didn't have the knowledge or capacity to run the country, I would answer that by the time they fought for it and won it they would have acquired the knowledge to run the country.

In fact this was one of my main arguments *for* direct democracy: that the process of fighting for it would bring into being the new persons – self-conscious, knowledgeable, self-reliant, self-governing, critical, thinking – envisaged by communism and that there was no other way this could be achieved. Here you have then a close intertwining of the goal and the strategy. Moreover, between the spring of 1969, when I first arrived at a fairly concrete image of communism, and November 1970, the draft constitution, there occurred: the New Mobe, the first and second general assemblies of the Committee of Returned Volunteers, the debates over Debray and over importing a guerrilla strategy, the endless debates on dozens of strategy questions like the focus on Washington, education versus fighting, the usefulness of mass rallies, electoral politics, the Weatherman/RYM II split, the Days of Rage and the Weatherman's Fall Offensive, plus all the strategy debates in CRV over church financing, the peace treaty, armed struggle, and so forth.

It is thus fairly inconceivable that strategy and goal could have been kept separate. What is probably more accurate to say is that the image of communism which I had fashioned in 1968-1969 served as a backdrop to all my subsequent debates about strategy. This probably accounts, for example, for my consistent opposition to the tendency to march on Washington at every crisis, as well as for my extreme ambivalence about mass demonstrations. It also helps account for our successful fight in June 1969 for the caucus structure in CRV as opposed to the coordinating committee arrangement, a fight, as now understood, against a democratic centralist structure (with a dash of pluralism thrown in through the more or less autonomous subcommittees) in favor of a council structure.

Other people haven't had this concrete image of communism in the back of their heads, or else have had a very different image of communism. A common view for example sees the revolution as the installation in Washington of a so-called socialist government. Hence my debates about strategy have often had a very perplexing and puzzling quality. My arguments have often not made a great deal of sense to other people. If, on rare occasion, the discussion has been calm enough and lasted long enough to finally work back to this basic starting for my position on any specific question of strategy, and it finally becomes clear to them that this is what undergirds my position, they often withdraw forthwith from the discussion, saying that this idea (the network of councils) is utopian or preposterous. That ends the debate with them because this is simply not a creditable position in their eyes.

This difficulty in communicating on concrete questions of strategy eventually convinced me that unless others had an image of the network of councils in their heads real communication with them was impossible. We only talked past each other. So I began trying to get the starting point out first and phrasing the whole issue in terms of the objective of the revolution – the party's seizure of power versus the proletariat's seizure of power. This was a much sounder approach, I think, and led to a real joining of the issues much faster, and usually brought the discussion to an end much quicker since if they rejected the council idea they naturally rejected also a strategy for achieving it.

The first time I can recall being confronted with the 'What do you do?' question was at the Black Panther sponsored Constitutional Convention in Washington, D.C. in November 1970. A friend had just finished reading the draft constitution I had written and said something to the effect that he didn't have any trouble with the image of socialism presented there but that I hadn't said a thing about ``what you do.'' He tended to dismiss the whole thing therefore as an academic exercise. That is, it didn't appear significant to him because the question of 'what you do' seemed to predominate in his mind. I remember how taken back I was by his response.

Two and a half years later in March 1973 I was confronted with this exact same question at the end of a two hour lecture-discussion at the Church Center for the United Nations. The question was asked by a person who admitted that he was oriented toward a vanguard party strategy, although he was interested in what I was saying. I had just finished demolishing the vanguard strategy piece by piece, beginning with the misplaced focus on anti-imperialism (common to both the Old Left and New Left), simultaneously outlining on the board in considerable detail a completely different conception of the revolution. And after all this then came the challenge: ``you haven't said a thing about what you do.''

I nearly flipped. On top of all that had just been said, the detailed outline on the board of the differing conceptions of the revolution, a whole list of characteristics of an egalitarian revolution, the explicit critique of vanguard strategy, the concrete description of the proletarian exercise of power – then the question `What do you do?' There was something very odd about this. There was obviously some truth to the question, but there was also a lot more to it than its truth. A few days before the March 1973 lecture, I now see in some miscellaneous notes, I had taken a new look at the question itself, as follows:

I think a breakthrough is emerging on the question of What do you do? which is what the vanguardists always ask. The very question is vanguardist. It presupposes a split between theory and action. The question is wrong somehow. This is the question I've been trying to answer and that's why I'm not getting anywhere. I've been trying to find tasks or activities that are thrown up by an egalitarian strategy. It is probably a question rather of the framework. Many of the specific activities would be the same but their meaning would be vastly different.

This is probably why this question struck me as out of order somehow. I pointed out the vanguardist implications of the question, and then added three new arguments:

(1) Redefining the goal, and the revolution itself, as I had done, was already of strategic significance, and in fact the whole argument that I had placed on the board was itself a strategy in a sense (the conception of winning a shift in decision-making out of bureaucracies in Washington into a network of councils for example).

(2) I had identified several features of a non-vanguard strategy comparable in every way to the so-called principles of the vanguard strategy (democratic centralism, discipline, and so forth) even though there were no labels for them yet, and the identification of such features already represented in outline form a whole strategy. Features like that:

> * The revolution must be made by the majority of the proletariat;
> * The revolution must be based on consciousness before the revolution;
> * The organizations of militants for various purposes must be distinguished from the organization of proletarians themselves for the purpose of collective

self-government;

* Proletarian democracy must be based on direct democracy not representative democracy;

* The revolution must focus on workplaces and aim at establishing a network of workers councils united on the basis of direct democracy;

* The revolution is in no sense inevitable and it makes no sense therefore to argue that proletarians lose because the situation isn't ripe; they lose that's all, because they haven't yet had, and may never have, sufficient forces to win;

* Proletarians must be prepared for war and be willing to use any means necessary in order to overthrow the ruling class;

* The revolution must reach its goal, a classless society;

* Even though a long historical process is necessary, the revolution, in the sense of the transfer of power from the bourgeoisie to the proletariat, will be a distinct, time-bound event.

(3) Finally, even if I hadn't said a thing about strategy, as he claimed, and even if the egalitarian image of the revolution I had presented seemed like an impossible dream, as he also claimed, and even if I couldn't at this time spell out the whole thing in complete detail, I said I wouldn't give up digging away at the

strategy question because everything else says that it has to be possible. This last point is a powerful one in fact. People say that a network of workers councils united on the basis of direct democracy is not possible. I say that everything says it has to be possible. A century of proletarian history and dozens of separate threads lead to it. If it is impossible then so also is the classless society. It has to work and there has to be a way of achieving it. It's like the missing piece of a puzzle. Once you have found it you know it has to fit because it is the only piece left. If at first it doesn't seem to fit you keep fooling around with it until finally it slips into place. That's why I don't stop pushing on the idea of a network of councils based on direct democracy. There are hundreds of bits and pieces of the problem that all point to this solution. It has to work because the rest of the overall configuration says it does.

Once again however, in this exchange, I never got beyond the preliminaries. In fact I remained on the defensive throughout. Rather than launching immediately into a description of the concrete egalitarian strategy, if that's what was wanted, I got bogged down in all these preliminaries. I get so engrossed in knocking down the vanguard strategy that there is never any time or energy left to spell out the alternative. A lot of the difficulty however, as even these brief comments show, is that the egalitarian strategy flows out of such a completely different framework that we can't even talk about it in the same way vanguardists talk about strategy. The vocabulary and concepts for it don't even exist. But it is also clear that the critique of vanguardism will never be effective until this is worked out, until a way is found to communicate across this breach.

For those who ask What do you do? the question seems natural enough, I suppose, whereas to me it seems peculiar, somehow beside the point, uncomprehending of what is being said, based on the duality, putting a misplaced priority on practice, flowing out of a distorted view of ends-means, and so forth. The only way to breach the gap, it seems to me, is to return to preliminary number one: why is the question What do you do? a vanguard question? This is the foundation upon which the bridge must be constructed.

Chapter Two

Why is the Question 'What Do You Do?' a Vanguard Question

---

*T*he question `What do you do?' presupposes that an activity (a doing) has a meaning in and of itself separate from the goal of that activity. This is not so. An activity derives its meaning from what it is intended to accomplish, from its aim. I usually cite several examples to demonstrate this:

(a) Two soldiers fighting each other on a battlefield may be engaging in exactly the same activities such as firing rifles, digging trenches, and using walkie-talkies. I don't understand the meaning of this activity however unless I can find out what they are fighting for. One soldier may be a freedom fighter and the other a fascist. They will both claim to be freedom fighters of course, so I will have to look more closely at the contents of their programs and make up my own mind which is which.

(b) Two militants may perform the same act – getting a job in a factory – in order to `join the working class' and `do factory organizing'. On the surface it looks like they are doing the same thing. But one may go into the factory as a petty bourgeois vanguardist, seeking to convert workers to the party line, to recruit them into the party, and to organize a mass base for the party's seizure of power. The other may go into the factory as an egalitarian proletarian militant for whom the main goal is the self-organization, self-emancipation, and self-government[3] of the working class – a militant who seeks to contest the power of the capitalist in the workplace by agitating for the establishment of democratic workers control over the workplace and the creation of a network of councils united on the basis of direct democracy. It is thus the goal or framework (the politics) of the person that gives meaning to the act of getting a job in a factory and doing workplace organizing.

(c) Consider the activity of talking with

---

3 The proletariat does not have a self. These expressions therefore are most inadequate. What they obviously imply is a collective organization and emancipation, but a collective form that is democratic and free and not something imposed from the outside. More on this as we proceed.

another person or persons, since the vanguard-ists never tire of admonishing that we should ``talk to the workers.'' If I am standing at a distance from two people engaged in conversation and cannot hear what is being said, I know precious little about the meaning of that activity. It all depends on what is being said, obviously. One person may be a member of the Ku Klux Klan, for all I know, seeking to recruit workers to that cause. Talking to a worker has no inherent

This is not a trivial point. Vanguardists constantly ignore, fail to recognize, or sweep under the rug (because they come at things from a dualistic point of view, putting the stress on practice) this element of consciousness or intention. This was brought home to me in a striking fashion the other day in a chance conversation with an old friend from the Columbia days. What has happened to her? She is now a member of Revolutionary Union, has left academia, has moved to the Midwest, and is putting out a local `working class' news-paper. She felt that she was now active, and doing practical work whereas in the university it was all academic.

But isn't this activity – newspaper work – mainly intellectual? Doesn't it deal with ideas? Does the activity of putting out a newspaper have any inherent meaning aside from the ideas printed in it? Obviously not. It depends on what is said in the newspaper. There is a newspaper for nearly every cause, however trivial. She did not stress this aspect, however, that the ideas being promulgated in the newspaper were good ideas that would help build toward revolution. Nor did she stress particularly the different category of people she was now conversing with (workers rather than students), although this aspect was of course there implicitly. What she stressed in her own description of herself was the `activity' of `putting out a newspaper' (and this was seen as working class and practical). This was her answer to my inquiry: ``what are you up to these days?''[4] Persons who are oriented like this will then turn right around and lay the whole party line thing on you, which is a theory obviously, all the while stressing their practice.

In the last analysis, organizing, in the vanguard mode, is primarily a question of winning allegiance, winning adherents, recruits, and converts, to this previously established intellectual doctrine. Acceptance of the doctrine is the basis for membership in the party and the basis of solidarity with others. And yet the vanguardists are always denouncing intellectuals. In their own eyes all this work involving ideas, concepts, abstractions, and so forth is seen as practice and is counterposed by them

---

4 It is a curious fact, just come to light, that I almost never ask people `what are you doing?', even as a greeting in this casual way. I say things like: what's up?, what's happening?, what's going on?, how are things?, and what are you up to?

to `petty bourgeois intellectualism'. What a weird thing. Even talking can be perceived by vanguardists as an activity (and one not involving consciousness) because consciousness and ideas are imported from the outside as fixed objects, as dogma, and are not seen, for example, as things that might emerge from the discussion itself or from the process of interaction. For them consciousness is a prior given: Marxism-Leninism.

This all flows out of the dualistic framework that undergirds their image of humans and the proletarian revolution. They do not understand Marx's central concept: labor. The split between being and consciousness, a split which Marx overcame in his concept of labor, permeates their entire outlook, and is central to all their main concepts: party/mass, leadership, discipline, theory/practice, organization, solidarity, criticism/self-criticism, and so forth. It is impossible for them to think naturally in terms of `Where are we going and how do we get there?' This is the real question. They ask instead: ``What is to be done?'' It is no accident that the real goal of the vanguardists, the party's seizure of power, is kept implicitly buried under the abstraction `seize power' and is pawned off as the proletariat's seizure of power. Nor is it an accident, given this dualistic blindness to the dialectic, to means-ends, to objective-subjective, to intention, to the essence of human labor as a world appropriating and world creating force, that the ultimate goal, communism, is left deliberately vague and undefined. In its place is put an indefinite transition period, a dark sea to be crossed under the aegis of the vanguard party.

The question `What do you do?' is a revealingly abridged one. My first impulse is always to ask, ``In order to do what?'' In the context of these discussions, it is obviously implicit that the question actually asks, ``What do you do in order to make the revolution?'' This is understood. Nevertheless, since the starting point is always `What do you do?', and not `How do you define the revolution?' (the goal) and then `What do you do to build it?', and since this latter point, the goal, is never raised concretely but is rather left vague and implicit, the stress on `What do you do?' has the effect of blocking praxis at the level of mindless activism.

No wonder it is so difficult, given all these obstacles, to examine whether the vanguard strategy really gets us to the goal: the classless society. Is it the right means for the desired end? Remember: knowledge is not something discovered and then applied. It is something *created*. Knowledge can be acquired only through human labor to meet some human need (goal, objective, end). I may very well have needs I don't know how to meet. I may feel a need to fly through the sky like a bird. But if I jump off a cliff with one of Leonardo's winged contraptions strapped to my back I may end up dead. On the other hand, if I flip a switch on a modern one-person jet propulsion system I may go soaring through the air.

Acquiring knowledge means to establish these real connections between the end and the means, between what I want and how I can get it. The end is an integral part of knowledge and can't be separated out. That is, I can't talk about knowledge as being only the means. It is the *connection* between means and ends that constitutes knowledge of the external world. And this knowledge can only be knowledge as appropriated for human purposes. It is not an objective knowledge because the subjective element, the human need (goal), is an integral aspect of this so-called knowledge of the external world. The two elements, subjective-objective, are inseparable.

In spite of surface similarities, this conception is a world away from the idea of practical know-how. For the ordinary pragmatist, know-how is divorced from the goal to be accomplished. The goal is imported from the outside. Policy (the goal) is left to the politicians or to the bosses, to the ruling class. Know-how is the *means* to accomplish any given goal. Thus knowledge is conceived dualistically, pertaining only to the means, not as above, dialectically, including both ends and means. Technicians separate values from facts, policy from know-how, principles from application. Values are not felt to be a part of knowledge (or of science) but come from elsewhere, from God, from the human condition, from leaders, or from politicians. They are, in a sense, arbitrary, at least as far as the technician is concerned. Thus we have applied engineering and applied engineers. We also have social engineers: neutral social scientists who decipher how society works so that the policy-makers can then achieve their goals.

A whole world is built up around this duality. It permeates every nook and cranny of the culture. In a recent interview with job placement counselors at Columbia University I was asked to make a list of activities that I had succeeded at and enjoyed doing. I was then asked to identify what aspect or function it was in each of these experiences that I enjoyed. As an example, looking at my list, they cited problem-solving as a function I appeared to enjoy. My reply was that Nixon had a great many problems that he badly needed solved but that I wasn't about to sign on. The whole approach of the counselors however was based upon a separation of the goal of an activity from these so-called functions (working with others, problem-solving, managing, writing, research). Their approach reflects, of course, and accepts, the present reality: the goal *is* given, by the employer, by the capitalist. My labor is only a means to his end. The counselors seemed to think that problem-solving could have some inherent meaning and satisfaction for me divorced from the problem that was being solved. This is what the capitalists would like, naturally. They want me to enjoy my job no matter what it is. So do the vanguard communists, by the way, who also ask me to be happy at even the dirtiest of jobs, but this time it is because I am `serving the people'. It is not surprising that counseling is an expanding occupation in an otherwise moribund culture.

There is something about Marxism-Leninism that prevents the establishment of these connections between ends and means, dialectically, as described above. Marxism-Leninism resembles far more the practical know-how of the technical expert. The goal in the Marxist-Leninist text is left very vague (``it's far too early to say what communism will look like").[5]Thus on the goal side we are in trouble. The goal is somehow taken out of the picture, swept under the rug, left implicit and unexamined, taken as a given, accepted on faith.

On the means side we are also in trouble. The strategy for achieving communism is set forth as a set of tried and tested principles (the accumulated wisdom of the working class, as interpreted by the party) and is placed beyond criticism or alteration because they are judged

---

5 Or else it is couched in double-talk, since the party's seizure of power is portrayed as the proletariat's seizure of power, even though this is a treacherous rock to try to stand on since it is a very unreal and implausible claim, a crude sleight-of-hand, to all but the true believers.

to have worked in the past. These principles –
democratic centralism, discipline, party/mass,
solidarity, criticism/self-criticism, leadership,
organization – are presented as fixed dogma,
encrusted by the lessons of seventy-five years
of struggle. Instead of working to clarify the
goal, therefore, and win agreement on it, and
then working to explore the means to effectively reach that goal, the Marxists-Leninists
somehow break the connection between the two
by burying the goal in various ways and then
elevating a fixed conception of the means to the
status of Thought, with a capital T.

This question of ends-means is a central one
and must not be handled in a mechanical fashion, like the vanguardists try to do. This is why
a response to the question `What do you do?'
cannot be a straightforward one. Everything
hinges upon whether a convincing argument
can be made that any given activity contributes
to the goal of achieving the classless society.[6]
By breaking the connection between ends and
means in the weird way they do, and by putting disproportionate stress on practice and

6 One would like to say ``and demonstrate in fact''
that the activity contributes to that end, but this demonstration in fact becomes a very complicated exercise
when the goal is the overthrow of a whole society and
the establishment of a new one, is something yet to
be achieved, and is something about which argument
will rage even after it happens over whether the goal,
communism, really resulted from the overthrow. So
the merits of a given strategy or activity can be judged
mainly on the basis of the case that can be marshaled
for or against it.

activity, vanguardists tend to treat means in a mechanical way. They overlook the fact that a means may reach an end in one situation but fail to in a different situation. This is how they can import the vanguard strategy from Russia, China, and Cuba into the United States without a second thought. That is, they neglect the total context, and hence necessarily the real connection between any given end and selected means.[7]

Vanguardists generally disparage, for example, working in the university, calling it petty bourgeois intellectualism. They say you should go get a job in a factory. Even here they continuously contradict themselves by making unadmitted, unrecognized exceptions for the Marxists-Leninists who work in the university and write books but who are seen as engaged in useful revolutionary work. It turns out therefore that they are not against professors as such, but only against bourgeois professors. Marxist-Leninist professors are apparently okay. But of course they never make this clar-

---

7 For a long time I have felt very uneasy with the claim, constantly reiterated by liberals, that the end does not justify the means. I suspect this must be very wrong, given its proponents, but I have never sat down to straighten it out. Recently I saw a reference to an article in Polish by Kolakowski entitled ``On the Validity of the Maxim that the End Justifies the Means.'' The maxim that the end does not justify the means certainly doesn't jive with the concept that revolutionary violence can be used to stop counter-revolutionary violence and to establish a society that is not founded on violence.

ification in their own thinking and continue to ridicule professors at large. This is what I mean by being mechanical. Whether or not a professor in a university is contributing to the revolution cannot be judged a priori, mechanically, but only by examining the content of that person's teaching and the consequences of their work there. This point should always be kept in mind even when the evidence is judged to show that most professors *are* reactionary. The same thing goes for any activity in the entire society, including workplace organizing. Workplace organizing may build toward revolution in one historical context and not in another.

Take another example. At the present time in the United States, given our conditions, I am against a focus on community organizing. I think it derails the revolution, pulling it away from the goal of a network of workers councils united on the basis of direct democracy. I think that this would be true under most conditions. But I would not want to say that it could never be justified, because someone may sometime be able to establish a plausible connection, under certain circumstances, between community organizing and the proletarian revolution.

I hope I'm not laboring the point. I probably am. But it is so central. It's the whole thing about the concrete examination of the concrete situation, a guideline the Marxists-Leninists say they endorse but in fact violate

all the time. They are walking violations of
that maxim. Consider the question of armed
struggle. Several years ago my circle of friends
went through a huge debate about armed
struggle. At that time there appeared to be
basically two sides: those against it (mainly
pacifists and those committed to civil disobedi-
ence as a strategy), and those for it. It appears
now however that among those who argued in
favor of armed struggle there was a further
split, buried. I argued for armed struggle but
for me it was a means we had to be willing to
use, and given the circumstances had better
count on having to use, in order to overthrow
the ruling class. Obviously it would be better if
it didn't have to be used. The pacifists on the
other hand rejected armed struggle as a matter of principle. That is what I was against in
their stance as much as their judgment that the
ruling class could be overthrown by peaceful
means. For the vanguardists (then latent, now
manifest) armed struggle was also a question of
principle, only they were for it, not against it
like the pacifists. Both groups took an absolute,
mechanical position. Vanguardists talk about
the *principle* of armed struggle and claim that
the revolution absolutely cannot be made without it. The thought that, under certain circumstances, it might be possible to overthrow the
ruling class without armed struggle, has been
purged even as a theoretical possibility from
their heads. This theoretical option was always

there for me, even though the probability of its actually happening has always seemed to be extremely low.

The Marxist-Leninist commitment to the *principle* of armed struggle is an excellent example of this mechanical treatment of means. One can go even further. Their very use of the term `principle' when referring to what is clearly only a means shows that for them the means has become the end, and is asserted dogmatically. Thus they expose their hopeless confusion. If the end is communism, then whether or not armed struggle is necessary to get there obviously depends on the circumstances. Let us say, though, that our concrete analysis of the circumstances convinces us that for the foreseeable future, for our historical era even, to think that a revolution can be made without armed struggle is the sheerest folly. This still does not mean that it becomes a Principle. It remains merely a means. But just try to argue a distinction like this, between armed struggle as a principle and armed struggle as an expediency, with the vanguardists and see how far you get. Either they will perceive your point as pacifist, and hence counter-revolutionary, or else they will consider it completely irrelevant and academic, and will push instead to ``get on with the job.'' (What job are we getting on with?) The possibility of a revolution without armed struggle may be only a remote one but its entertainment marks the difference between the dogmatist and the dialectician, and this is the same difference that distinguishes revolutionaries from counter-revolutionaries, proletarians from bourgeoisie, authoritarians from democrats.

To be thorough about this we would have to go through a similar line of reasoning for each of the specific strategy debates that have split the movement in recent years. And what if we did? To take one more example, what if, say, we decided that for now, at this time and in this place, electoral politics was an indefensible strategy to win proletarian power? We would then have to be willing to continuously reexamine that policy in light of changing circumstances. If we never reach a decision on strategy we can never move anywhere. If we don't constantly reexamine each item of strategy we will also never move, certainly not very far. This seems to me essential in order to have *any* intelligent, nondogmatic position on any question of strategy. This much is commonplace. Dogmatism, however, as I will attempt to show further on, involves a lot more than simply failing to continuously reexamine a position in light of new developments. Everyone, after all, claims to make a concrete analysis of the situation and to base their proposed strategy on that analysis. I certainly do. I have a whole list of positions on strategy which I could reel off if asked, ``What do you do?'' (but they are different in quality from vanguard positions, even if outwardly the same, because of their epistemological base). I feel quite strongly about most of these points. It is obviously over issues like these that people split. Thus I am certainly not trying to say that everything is relative, or that people should never take a stand on the issues. That is the pluralist position, not mine.

My answer to `What do you do?' would begin first of all with a long list of don'ts:

- don't be a Jesus freak or a follower of Maharaj Ji
- don't be a pacifist
- don't join PL, RU, SWP, OL, YAWF, or any Old Left group
- don't play around with astrology
- don't pour your energies into electoral politics
- don't organize youth, women, and Third World People
- don't define the enemy as imperialism
- don't focus on community organizing
- don't bother with food coops or free clinics
- don't peddle crafts to the counterculture
- don't say you have to be gay to be revolutionary
- don't go back to the farm
- don't go underground to harass the empire from the inside

- don't start an organic food restaurant
- don't be an academic Marxist
- don't try to be both radical and Christian
- don't try to build a vanguard party
- don't fight to get men out of power and women into power
- don't join a rural commune
- don't be an organizer
- don't read from the Little Red Book
- don't be a Woodstock nation counterculture freak
- don't try to work from within the establishment
- don't drop out
- don't petition the government
- don't embrace Marxism-Leninism-Mao-Tse-Tung Thought
- don't serve the people
- don't stay zonked on dope
- don't throw away your matches

This is a start certainly but like I say, in order to be meaningful, each of these positions would have to be examined and defended in detail. When and where? For how long? Why? And so forth. For those who are trying to decide what to do with their lives it is the detailed examination and defense of any one of these that matters, that is, the rationale. For militants the whole problem is to establish a rationale for one's revolutionary work. It must be possible to see a connection between one's life energies and the hoped for victory of the revolution. Actually, for many militants, the `What do you do?' question is really the `What do I do with my life?' question. That is, how do I spend it, use it, to the best advantage? The dilemma may be between working in a factory or office or becoming a union or party official or teaching in the university or going underground, and so on. The need is to develop a defense for one or the other option, a judgment about the consequences or meaning of the various choices, a justifiable belief that a given course of activity will lead to the desired liberation. Thus the intentional dimension, the connection between ends and means, cannot be suppressed even when it is buried under the dualistic terminology. My life is not synonymous with my `activity'. If that were so then I would be nothing but a mere means, all of me. My goal after all, to escape wage-slavery, is not something imposed upon me from the outside. It is my very own. My life has meaning only in the connection between my own means (activities) and my own ends (goals). They are both inside of me and can in no way be separated, even if I wanted to do so.

This is why I never ask `What do you do?' My questions are `Where are we going?' and `How do we get there?' I have advanced a concrete answer to the first question by asserting that the goal of the revolution is to establish a network of workers councils united on the basis of direct democracy, a set of relationships which would, if ever achieved, constitute the exercise of proletarian power, and be an embodiment and expression of an egalitarian, classless society, and hence of freedom. This form is not in itself a foolproof guarantee of egalitarian relations, but at least it makes them possible. Domination can perpetuate itself in spite of the most democratic procedures imaginable, however, so I am not merely talking about a form or a constitution, but about real changes in the quality of the relationships.

In any case, the council idea at least provides a concrete answer to the question about where we are going. The question which remains to be answered is 'How do we get there?' Having finally finished with the preliminaries, I can now turn to this, the starting point. Perhaps the best way to proceed here is to try to reconstruct, as above, the history of my own confrontation with these problems, although this might best be topically organized rather than chronologically. This should go fairly smoothly because I think these deliberations fall easily into three or four distinct topics.

Chapter Three
The Proletariat and Protagonists of the Proletariat

*A*round the time of the second *Telos* conference in November 1971, I started arguing that there were three legitimate niches for radicals: (a) direct participation in workplace struggles at one's own place of work; (b) participation outside the workplace in a local group having direct links to real workplace struggles, in some assisting capacity; or (c) participation in a propaganda or media group seeking to publicize the struggles of these first two groups.

I think this three-niche argument is basically sound but I have since simplified it into a two-niche scheme: the proletariat and the protagonists of the proletariat. One very helpful insight was Martin Glaberman's comment at the *Telos* conference that we shouldn't confuse the organizations radicals create in order to go about their work of agitation with the self-organization of proletarians for the purpose of collective self-government. Another useful insight was the recognition of the disjunction between class position and class orientation. One can be a wage-laborer but not have a proletarian outlook. Conversely, one can have a proletarian outlook but not be a wage-laborer. Moreover, the acquisition of a proletarian outlook is not simply a matter of becoming a wage-laborer in the objective sense of class position. Petty bourgeois organizers who get jobs in factories to vanguard the revolution remain petty bourgeois in outlook even though they become wage-laborers in terms of their position in the structure. They still haven't managed to get inside the proletariat even though they have managed to get inside a factory.

Nevertheless it is important that we not therefore attempt to make the proletariat synonymous with all those who seek and believe in the proletarian revolution, i.e., with all those who are inside the proletarian class outlook. This might seem convenient and desirable to some. It would mean however that the proletarian outlook would then be nothing more than a religion and the proletariat merely a religious body, admitting as members all those who subscribe to the dogma. This would be nice if it weren't for the fact that the society has (according to our theory) a certain structure, certain relations of production, relations which cannot be changed by just anyone. Only certain people are in a position in the structure to overthrow the ruling class. (Whether they ever try to or not is another question).

If the revolution is understood as the proletarian seizure of power through the establishment of a network of workers councils united on the basis of direct democracy, then it is clear that only people who are wage-laborers in workplaces (offices, factories, fields, stores, restaurants, shops, and so forth) are in a position to set up these councils and participate directly in the seizure of power and the establishment of a proletarian decision-making apparatus. A small farmer, for example, or a child, or a self-employed dentist, or a housewife, or a retired person, or a welfare recipient, is not in a position to participate directly in this process, however much they may assist in other capacities.[8]

This is only true, obviously, if the revolution is defined as the proletariat's seizure of power. It is not true in the vanguard strategy, where the revolution is seen as the party's seizure of

---

8 After the event, nearly all these people will become workers in a council – everyone perhaps except the young, the sick, the retired, and the imprisoned, and even their exclusion is not necessarily unavoidable, nor warranted.

power by its capture of the capitalist institutions of government and their functions (like decision-making) with the support of a `mass base' made up of a coalition of `all oppressed peoples' held together by `solidarity'. What it actually is that holds all these groups together is allegiance to the dogma and discipline of the party, that is, to the party's conception of the revolution. This is why Marxism-Leninism *is* a religion in the bourgeois and prebourgeois mold, not a new and revolutionary world outlook. Solidarity in the Marxist-Leninist dictionary is only a fancy word for that age-old cohesive force that binds together any religious group into a solid mass.

The small farmer, the intellectual, the lumpen, the small-time capitalist, even the bourgeois, can fight in the vanguard army/ party in support of the party's seizure of power as easily as the wage-laborer can. Thus, in spite of all the hullabaloo the vanguard makes about the proletariat leading the revolution, the proletariat's position in the alliance and the function assigned to it in the fight, under the vanguard strategy, is actually no different than, and on an equal footing with, other elements of the alliance: they are all part of the mass base which pours out into the streets for mass demonstrations on cue. What you have to do to get into the proletarian revolution in the vanguard version is subscribe to Marxism-Leninism as interpreted by the Central Committee. This is what holds the alliance of all oppressed peoples together: dogma and discipline. If the revolution can be made by all oppressed people, regardless of their position in the society, then it is no wonder that it is felt that some force must exist to link all these groups together and weld them into a fighting force, a good job for a self-proclaimed leadership. Fortunately, the only kind of revolution that can be made with dogma and discipline is a bourgeois revolution, not a proletarian one.

It is easy to see why and how, given this analysis, that vanguardists tend to define racial or ethnic minorities in a country as 'nations' to be welded together by the party into a multinational revolution against imperialism. I might also note in passing that the import of Althusser's Marxism is precisely this: it is a theory which calls for welding together all these oppressed elements into a hegemonic block. This is also why the strategy writings of the NLR group (Blackburn, Anderson, et al) reek so with elitism. It is this structuralist thing. If you understand the structure then you can weld it together to overthrow capitalism. The welders of course are the Marxists-Leninists.

The distinction between the proletariat and the protagonists of the proletariat is thus more important than it appears at first sight. It helps to clarify a number of very thorny issues. Consider the dilemma faced by persons who believe in and seek the proletarian revolution but who are not themselves wage-laborers, a person like Marx for example. What is the role of such people in the revolution? It is clear that they cannot make the revolution directly themselves because they are not in a position to do so. They don't even work at a workplace (a capitalist workplace) where they could help seize the means of production and help establish ``an association of free and equal producers,'' to use Marx's phrase. They certainly cannot take over someone else's workplace. A workplace can only be occupied and defended by those who work in it. This is why the emancipation of proletarians can only be accomplished by themselves, something which is not true in the vanguard strategy where it is conceivable, and is in fact common, that oppressed classes other than the proletariat (e.g., peasants) can constitute a sufficient enough base to enable the party to seize power. The party then presides (or so the theory goes) over the emancipation of the proletariat in the so-called transition to communism.

Marx, on the other hand, always insisted that proletarians had to emancipate themselves. He put this as the first principle in the bylaws of the IWA. I do not believe that Marx ever considered himself a leader of the proletarian revolution, in the sense that present day vanguardists use this term. He always talked instead about his *agitation*. That's what he was

doing in 1848. That's what he did in London.
He talked about agitation, about the critique
of bourgeois society, about the proletariat's
emancipation of itself, not about his leadership of the proletariat. This is how he fought.
There was never any question of his leading
a party to take over the state. The IWA was
essentially a propaganda organization. Marx
dedicated his major work to his friend Wil-
helm Wolff, an ``intrepid, faithful, noble protagonist of the proletariat.'' Marx ridiculed
even Bakunin and his followers, paradoxically
enough, for their *elitism*:

> Thus the autonomous workers'
> sections are in a trice converted
> into *schools*, of which these gen-
> tlemen of the Alliance {Bakunin,
> et al} will be the masters. They
> *evolve the idea* by "consistent
> studies" which leave no trace
> behind. They then "*carry* this
> idea to our workers organiza-
> tions." To them, the working
> class is so much raw material,
> a chaos into which they must
> breathe their Holy Spirit before
> it acquires a shape.[9]

This cannon ball of Marx's broadside against
elitism is conveniently overlooked by the van-

---

9 From "Ficitious Splits in the International," by
Carl Marx and Friedrich Engels; written March 1872
and published in Geneva 1872 as a French pamphlet
called *Les Pretendues Scissions dans l'Internationale.*

guardists. If I am not a wage-laborer, fighting at my own place of work to seize power there, then I am (if I am a revolutionary) a protagonist, a fighter in the cause for, that self-emancipation, and this can be done in innumerable ways.

I would go further and say that even for people who are wage-laborers structurally speaking, to the extent that their efforts are not at their own places of work but outside them they are also essentially protagonists of the proletariat. They are not in those particular efforts directly involved in the struggle for workers control and the appropriation of the means of production but are rather advocating such a course and agitating for it in the community or society at large. If I already am a wage-laborer, then obviously the key task for me is the occupation and defense of my workplace and the establishment of a democratic council there linked up with other councils across the land. It is only a question of when and how. But it may very well be, for any number of reasons, that such a struggle is not on the agenda momentarily at my own workplace. In such a case being a protagonist of the proletarian revolution in nonworking hours outside the workplace is obviously better than doing nothing at all.

If I am not a wage-laborer however the question of whether to become one on purpose by deliberately getting a job in a factory or office is more complicated. This depends on the circumstances, on the stage of the revolution, the size of the proletarian movement, the clarity of its goals, my own skills and background, and on a host of other considerations. If there is little movement in factories and offices, if the proletarian outlook is weak, or if most of the radicals agitating in the factories are petty bourgeois vanguardists, then it may be a foolish course of action and a waste of time and effort. Perhaps very little could be accomplished there toward building the revolution. Perhaps more could be accomplished elsewhere.

It is clear that if struggles for councils and for workers control in factories and offices never take place a proletarian revolution will never be made. However, the preconditions for such struggles on a widespread and sustained basis are much less clear. Going in to start a fight at any given time in any given factory or office may or may not be a wise thing. And this is a particularly difficult judgment it seems to me for anyone who is `going in' for that express purpose. If I am there already, if that is my life anyway, I am a lot more likely to know what can be done toward taking the place over and when and how. It is only the vanguardists, who think mechanically about everything, who aim not at the proletariat's emancipation of itself but rather at the construction of the Marxist-Leninist Party and a mass movement, who are apparently not even aware of the dialectic, who simultaneously romanticize and patronize the working class, who confuse being inside a factory with being inside the proletariat, who see themselves as welding together an alliance of all oppressed people according to the scientific principles of Marxism-Leninism, it is only people like this who feel that getting a job in a factory can be easily equated with building toward revolution.

But of course it is not merely their working inside a factory that gives them a sense of meaning and a sense of movement toward revolution. It is the factory work in combination with their membership in the Party. Joining the working class and joining the Party usually go hand in hand. Radicals like this usually seek mainly to recruit workers into the party and to win converts to Marxism-Leninism, and it is this I suspect that makes getting a factory job a plausible decision in their eyes. The long struggle for democratic workers control of the workplace and the extremely difficult and pioneering effort needed to establish a network of councils could not possible sustain them. Only wage-slaves who are already there as a matter of course, who are trapped there, so to speak, will have the strength to sustain such a fight, not outsiders, not would-be workers and bogus radicals from the petty bourgeoisie.

Nevertheless, this is not to say that becoming a wage-laborer might not be the right thing to do under certain circumstances, if one is not one already like most people are, and if there is a choice in the matter. It is the framework within which this is done that counts more than anything.

Chapter Four

If it is Dogmatic to Fight to Build a Vanguard Party Why Isn't It Just as Dogmatic to Fight to Establish a Network of Councils?

*T**his is the festering question buried* in the previous sections which I want to dig up right now and expose to the light. Otherwise it will plague us from here on out. On the one hand I claim that anyone going into a factory to recruit people into the Marxist-Leninist vanguard party remains bourgeois in class outlook and fails to get inside the proletariat even though they are inside the factory. On the other hand I claim that this is not so for the person who goes in to start a fight to establish a network of workers councils united on the basis of direct democracy. This person is a genuine proletarian revolutionary I argue. How can this be? Don't both persons put forth a program and fight for it? Don't they both have a line? Aren't they both therefore equally dogmatic? (The answer is no.) This is one of the thorniest issues I have ever dealt with. So far it has been next to impossible for me to get across to others the distinction that I make between these.

Liberals, seeing that I have a program, and that I take a strong stand on the issues and fight to defend my position, say that council communists are therefore just as sectarian and dogmatic as Marxists-Leninists. The vanguardists, seeing these things, say that I have a line just like they do, but that it is the wrong line. They therefore reject the charge of dogmatism that I have directed against them, proceed to define me as counter-revolutionary, and try to drive me out of the workplace. `Dogmatic' in fact is not a meaningful concept for vanguardists, nor is sectarian or petty bourgeois, all of which are for them merely pejorative terms used to denigrate those who disagree with their own line. I cannot hope to completely unravel this thorny problem here, but perhaps I can try to catch the essence of the solution to it, which it seems to me is now possible to see.

The first germ of the solution to the problem emerged for me in the spring of 1972 after the split at the *Liberated Guardian* and the fight over the statement interpreting that split. It was then that I made the connection between the Network of Councils idea as formulated in my draft constitution of November 1970 (and consequently the whole problem of democracy in a proletarian society) and the critique of positivism (bourgeois science, objectivity, value-free social science) that had been emerging also but separately. This insight got its first solid statement in the initial essay on Hinton in February 1973.

Until this new bead on the question of dogmatism started emerging after March 1972 my answer to this kind of objection (Aren't you both dogmatic?) was that elitism (vanguardism, dogmatism), as distinct from an egalitarian strategy, had nothing to do with whether someone fought or not or took the initiative. Rather, the two roads, bourgeois and proletarian, had to do with *what* was being fought for and could therefore be distinguished only by examining the contents of the different programs. The following paragraph is a fairly typical expression of this position.

Once the image is grasped of the revolution as a vast takeover of workplaces and the reorga-

nization of the society into a network of workers councils based on direct democracy then the
whole problem of the vanguard disappears (as
a theoretical problem that is). To be in revolt
and to try to get others to revolt does not necessarily turn a person or group into a vanguard,
not if they are inside the working class, just as
taking the initiative to achieve the revolution
does not necessarily mean that a worker is an
elitist. If you start a fight with the ruling class
that doesn't make you an elitist. That merely
means that you have become conscious of your
oppression and are trying to end it. Others will
ask what you are doing. They may join you, or
oppose you, or stand on the sidelines a while
longer. What is going on here is the emergence
of the self-consciousness of the proletariat and
the capacity for self-government. The difference between an elitist and a nonelitist is not
that one takes the initiative while the other
does not. If that were so then there would be
no alternative to elitism except passivity. Not
wanting to be a leader and dominate, a person
would have no option but to be a follower and
submit. Obviously there must be a third possibility if the duality is to be transcended. Clearly, the difference between a vanguard strategy
and an egalitarian strategy lies in the goal of
the revolution that is being fought for, whether
merely to defeat capitalism or to establish an
egalitarian society,[10] and the way in which it is

10 When this was written I had not yet come

fought for, whether in a condescending manner from the outside or in an egalitarian manner from the inside, and not with whether or not a battle is waged to make it.[11]

This seems to be a pretty good answer to the question until it is noted that it overlooks one crucial fact: all radicals claim to be revolutionary, democratic, proletarian, nonsectarian, and nonelitist. The people I call vanguardists and petty bourgeois, bogus radicals see themselves as real revolutionaries and their program as genuinely proletarian, and see me as counter-revolutionary. There is obviously a disagreement about what the proletarian outlook is. There is even disagreement about who is in the proletarian class, leaving aside the question of consciousness.

My statement above overlooks this disagreement and presupposes that there is some objective way to establish that the content of my program is democratic while the content of their program is authoritarian, that the content of my program is proletarian while the content of theirs is bourgeois. Actually, all factions claim to be democratic and proletar-

to regard Russia as a full blown capitalist country, regarding it instead as some sort of unnamed hierarchical bureaucratic monster (a la Trotsky I subsequently learned), and hence labored to make a distinction between overthrowing capitalism and achieving communism.

11 From the piece, ``What Kind of Working Class Politics?,'' which appears as the postscript to my essay *Coming to Terms with the New Left*.

ian. We are faced with a situation therefore where everyone says, ``Give me liberty or give me death,'' and where all parties to the conflict claim to be fighting for liberty. This is true for the conflict between the proletariat and the bourgeoisie as well as for the splits within the movement to overthrow the bourgeoisie.

Liberals, when confronted with a situation like this, say, ``We are right but we don't want to impose our views on you, so you do your thing and we'll do ours'' (and live together in love and harmony). This is obviously an impossible stance, and only an illusion. What it means in effect, since they abstain from voting to establish a common policy, declaring themselves neutral and rejecting even the coercive force of majority rule, is that policy will be set by others. It is no wonder then that liberals/individualists withdraw to the shelter of their imaginary sanctuaries inside their walled universities and remote rural communes. There they devise whole philosophies to justify this pretension, using concepts like the separation between fact and value, scientist and policy maker.

Vanguardists, when confronted with a situation like the above, say unhesitatingly, ``We are right.'' Why? ``Because we have the Correct Strategy as determined by the science of Marxism-Leninism.'' They furthermore assert that as soon as they are able to seize power others will do it their way or else.

Proletarians, when confronted with such a situation, say, ``We are right.'' But they do not claim that this is based on objective fact, scientific knowledge, Absolute Truth, the Authority of Marx and Lenin, or a Correct Strategy. Rather, they recognize their position for what it is: the best *judgment* that they are able to make of the available evidence and possible options. It is also based however upon a recognition of the necessity of choosing (of voting to establish policy) if they are not to forfeit their control over their own lives or acquiesce in letting others pick which road to take.

Perhaps I can state more clearly now why the Network of Councils is not a dogmatic program whereas the Vanguard Party is. The idea of a network of workers councils united on the basis of direct democracy is a conception of the proletarian exercise of power which is based upon the recognition that there is no outside, objective way to determine what the correct road is. It is based squarely on the dialectic, not on the bourgeois duality. In fact, it is the strategic embodiment of the dialectic. It is a program that brings everyone into the decision-making process on an equal footing. It is a program that gives every worker a voice in the determination of basic policy, where every worker becomes a thinking person with power to judge the issues for themselves, with disagreements being resolved by majority rule.

If the majority were in fact in power then the notion of dogmatism would lose all meaning, as would the idea of a struggle over the socialist road. *Every* vote would be a struggle over the correct policy. The minority on any given issue might claim that the majority was taking the road back to capitalism or that the majority's position was a dogmatic one, but then, the minority is not in power. Who is to decide? Issues are decided by majority rule.

Even the question of whether the majority is in fact in power is a question of judgment and hence of potential disagreement. We hardly need recall that the majority of people in the United States today believe, after a fashion (or at least they did until quite recently), that the majority is already in power here and that the United States is a democratic society. It is entirely probable that even if a network of councils and direct democracy were established some group or other would charge that such an arrangement didn't represent democratic workers control at all, or perhaps would argue that majority rule had never in fact been established in the first place,[12] and would therefore agitate for that or for some other system, say a Communist Party with a Central Committee and a Chairman, claiming that this was real

12 They would thus occupy a position similar to the one held by radicals in the United States today, vis-a-vis the majority, in arguing that the U.S. is not a democracy and never has been.

democracy. If the minority decided to bolt, that would be counter-revolution from the point of view of the majority, revolution from the viewpoint of the minority. Was the majority already in power as it claimed or was the established arrangement merely a sham, as charged by the rebels. This is the judgment that each worker would have to make in deciding whether to join those in power (who claim to be in the majority) to suppress the rebels or join the rebels (who also claim to be in the majority or at least to have its backing, for how else could they justify themselves?) to overthrow those in power.

It is abundantly clear therefore that the fight between the authoritarian and the democratic tendencies, the vanguard party freaks and the council communists, the bogus radicals and the real revolutionaries, the oppressors and the oppressed, the tyrants and the freedom fighters, is an unending one. There will always be some jerk trying to run the whole show, all in the name of democracy and freedom. Freedom can never be achieved once and for all, but is something continuously won and defended through endless vigilance against those seeking to pass minority rule off as majority rule. And there is no way under the sun to determine objectively which is which. Everyone claims to be a freedom fighter and on the side of right, even capitalists. All I can do is examine the claims, arguments, actions, and consequences of each tendency, try to make up my own mind, try to persuade others that I am right, and hope that the majority will come down on the same side I do (or respect my right to dissent if they don't).

Once we see that virtually any difference between two people about which way to go (policy) is potentially a class difference and hence a question of class struggle (the road to freedom versus the road to slavery), then it becomes clear that the only way the class struggle can be joined is through the fight to establish majority rule in a network of workers councils united on the basis of direct democracy and the subsequent struggle between the majority and the minority in those councils over the correct policy. Any other strategy leads to a situation where only some of the people get to decide what it means to be proletarian and on the road to socialism. This has to be the heart of the revolution given the fact that there is no outside, objective way to determine what the socialist road is, but only a question of my judgment against yours.

Thus the attempt to separate `contradictions among the people' from `contradictions with the enemy' is doomed from the start because it presupposes an outside authority (the party) to define who the enemy is as opposed to the people. If it is true (and it is) that any fork in the road holds the possibility of leading forward to communism and freedom or backward to capitalism and slavery then any difference between you and me, no matter how trivial it may seem at first, holds the potential of a split, where we each take a different way, where each of us defines the road taken by the other as capitalist, and where, therefore, we become enemies.[13]

And this is the way it should be. Judgments like these cannot be left to the Central Committee. I want to have a chance to present my views on which way to go on an equal footing with others, and to hear what they have to say as well – to listen to and to be listened to – so that everyone can hear what the issues are and try to make up their own minds. It is this, the inherent openness, and the *inclusion of everyone's voice*, that permits us to claim that the council strategy is nondogmatic whereas the

---

13 In the society at large, say in relations between friends, or in families, communes, or voluntary organizations such splits can lead to complete breaks in relationships and to severance of ties, a possibility which exists because these relations are only partial ones within a framework of fragmentation and atomization, with the overall social cohesion being imposed from above. It is only in workplace struggles that opportunity exists for a different dynamic to emerge regarding splits, and a different outcome. The fight for majority rule in the workplace, leading as it can to majority rule in the entire society through a Network of Councils, is thus the key to the question of splits and to the establishment of a new relationship between the revolutionary minority and the counter-revolutionary majority (or vice versa, depending on whether one is in the minority or the majority, obviously), and to an entirely new perception of and relationship to the heretic.

vanguard strategy isn't.

Sectarianism (dogmatism) is thus not merely an intellectual phenomenon. It is not merely the habit of mind that fails to keep an analysis up-to-date, fails to make a concrete analysis of the concrete situation, hiding instead behind ossified abstractions and rigid formulas that are not rooted in real life. That is, dogmatism is not merely the mental outlook that confuses the concrete and the abstract and botches the link between the two. Dogmatism is all this but is not only this. It is also, perhaps even primarily, the *exclusion of others from decision-making*. This is what turns people into sectarians. This is what makes them blind to disagreements (unseeing, in the sense of not listening). Thus blinded they are able to pretend that their own views are correct, and for objective reasons. They are able to pretend that their views are universal, true, and timeless, characteristics which they think justifies the imposition of these views on everyone else.

Sectarianism is thus preeminently a class phenomenon, and hence in our time it is a bourgeois phenomenon. It is based on power. It is a political thing, not merely an intellectual disease. Sectarianism flows out of the bourgeoisie's appropriation of power to itself and the exclusion of others from power, an appropriation which enables it to pretend to be above society and outside history, and to speak for the entire society rather than merely for itself.

Nothing establishes the true credentials of the Old Left more firmly than the sorry spectacle of dozens of strident, fanatic Marxist-Leninist sects, shouting it out, trying to establish the correctness of their lines, as determined objectively and scientifically, and as sanctioned by the authority of Marx. These are not proletarian voices. They are the voices of the bourgeoisie in radical guise.

The vanguardists of course reject the claim that there is no objective way of determining what the radical policy is. Their whole strategy is based upon the belief that there is such a possibility. Thus the conflict between the vanguardists and the egalitarians is joined long before we ever reach the disputes between the majority and minority on the shop floor. The dispute is over whether to even fight for a council in the first place, and whether the councils are the central element rather than a party. In the last analysis my claim that there is no objective way of choosing the socialist road is a question of judgment. That's my reading of the situation. But then so is their claim that there is an objective way to determine the socialist road. That is their reading. This is surely one of the most powerful arguments in favor of the council strategy, since it is built on and designed for disagreement, as well as agreement. The vanguard strategy is designed only for agreement (solidarity).

But of course the vanguardists deny that

their belief in objectivity is only a question of their judgment and hence a matter of disagreement. They say it is a Fact and therefore True. So round and round we go. I can only hope that eventually most people will come down on the side of the council strategy. This does not seem to be happening at the moment however. Marxism-Leninism appears to be spreading like wildfire, along with a dozen other forms of `mysticism', like astrology, Christianity, science, and gurus of every description. I'm afraid the politics I represent will remain a weak minority position in the immediate future. It seems to me however that there are reasons to be optimistic that Marxism-Leninism will burn out in the long run, but this is not the place to try to explain why. It is in any case not inevitable.

We would have to examine proletarian epistemology (the dialectic), as well as the class origins of dualism, in much more depth to get any firmer grip on this issue. I believe that things like dogmatism and proselytizing do exist, but they flow out of the duality, not the dialectic. If you reject this distinction however and this conception of knowledge, then we are nowhere; or rather, we are right back where we started: in a political struggle for power. It's like the struggle between the bourgeoisie and the proletariat. The proletariat says that it is exploited and oppressed, held in slavery. The bourgeoisie claims that everyone is free and equal, that we are all citizens in a democratic

society. These are two irreconcilable inter-
pretations of the same reality. Which is true?
The question of truth hardly even has any rel-
evance. It is a question of which prevails. As
long as most wage-laborers remain convinced
(with a little help from the bourgeoisie) that
they are free and equal citizens, the proletarian
view remains a submerged, ineffectual, minority outlook.[14]

The situation is similar in the conflict
between the authoritarian and democratic tendencies in the radical movement. Even after I
expose and refute the content of the Marxist-
Leninist program I find that vanguardists go
right on being vanguardists. The conflict must
be fought out in the political arena. It is a fight
to prevail, to win, and to muster sufficient
forces to win, which for the most part boils
down to getting enough people on the side I am
on, on the side of council communism. This is
the road to socialism. But this cannot be established as objective, scientific truth. It is merely
my judgment. It is fortunate that there *is* no
foolproof way to tell who the freedom fighters
really are. If there were a way there would be no
need to think. As it is, each person has to examine the three main roads (and all other roads)
and make up their own minds about which road
leads to communism. Right prevails only in the

14 This holds also for Russia, China, Cuba, Vietnam, and Korea, where apparently most people are
convinced that their countries are already communist.

eyes of the winners. For the losers, defeat is always a tragic setback for the correct view.

I believe that the image of the proletarian exercise of power that is embodied in the notion of a network of workers councils united on the basis of direct democracy brings the reality of these disagreements to the fore where they can be dealt with. It highlights the connection between human labor, consciousness, and the creation of the future human reality. If a network of councils based on direct democracy were ever brought into being the link between consciousness and human social reality would finally be made. Under the bourgeoisie, and under the Party as well, this connection is camouflaged, hidden, mystified. Behind the screen of mystery the power of capital continues unthreatened and the slavery of labor continues unabated.

I hope to return to this whole question of sectarianism (especially as it pertains to the majority/minority struggle within workplace councils) in a later essay on the dynamics of workplace struggles. The workplace is obviously the key arena, and the struggle there has moved more and more to the center for me, catching as it does in a very concrete way the many arguments about the tactics and strategy of the revolution. The workplace arena is absolutely central for example to the solution of the problem of splits. An essay on the dynamics of workplace struggles therefore will be needed to complete even a tentative answer to the question about how we get there. But for now I want to set this aside and deal next with several matters external to the workplace struggle.

Chapter Five
How Do We Agitate for the Proletariat's Emancipation of Itself?

*L*eaving to one side the problems faced by militants agitating on the shop floor for the establishment of a council, let me examine the situation of nonwage-laborers (or wage-laborers for whom effective agitation in their own workplaces is out of the question) who want to agitate for the proletarian revolution. How do these protagonists of the proletariat agitate for the self-emancipation of the proletariat? I have already established at least a partial basis for answering this question. Perhaps I should briefly recapitulate this starting point. For the purposes of the present discussion, the two most pertinent points made so far are: (a) that the revolution must be made by the majority of the proletariat, and (b) that the revolution must be based on consciousness *before* the revolution. What this says is that the proletarian revolution cannot be made *for* the proletariat by a vanguard minority, even if supported by uprisings of the mass base. If the revolution is made by a minority in the majority's name then it is not a proletarian revolution, but a bourgeois revolution. It is a characteristic of bourgeois revolutions that they are minority revolutions made in the name of the entire society.

If the revolution is made by the proletarian majority itself then there is no way that this can be an unconscious revolution. Obviously, the proletarians must be aware that they are making a revolution. They must consciously intend to do so. They must know what they are doing, have plans and strategies, and have a blueprint for how to reorganize things and exercise power. The Proletarian Revolution, by its very nature, cannot be a blind, accidental, or unintended event. The idea that proletarians can make a revolution and then exercise power without a prior plan for doing so is one of the grossest absurdities of vanguard politics and betrays more than anything else the real intentions of vanguardists, which is to exercise power themselves in the name of proletarians. As long as the proletarian majority does not take it upon itself to emancipate itself (and the proletariat can be emancipated in no other way) there is nothing anyone can do about it, except agitate for that self-emancipation.

It might be useful here to draw an analogy between the problem of the proletarian revolution and the problem of the immature, dependent person. There is absolutely nothing anyone can do to force a person to grow up and become mature, independent, and self-reliant. You can tell a person to grow up. You can advocate self-reliance, withdraw support, deny dependent requests, and criticize immature behavior. But there is no way that you can actually stop these things and create maturity in another person. That person either achieves maturity alone or not at all. It cannot be done *for* the person. A protagonist of maturity therefore is actually in a rather limited position, which is usually a very frustrating one as well. A protagonist of self-reliance can do many things to try to prod a person into it, but is, in the last analysis, quite helpless when it comes to the actual creation of that capacity in the dependent person. It can't be done from the outside, by others. The very aim, the objective to be accomplished, precludes forcing a person to be mature. It is impossible, by definition. It is not something that can be done for another person. And to try to force self-reliance is synonymous with abandoning the goal.

The vanguardists have never learned this lesson. In their stance toward the proletariat, vanguardists presume that proletarian emancipation can be forced, and that it can be accomplished by an outside force – the party, leaders, intellectuals, revolutionaries – whereas in reality it can only be accomplished from the inside by the proletariat itself. This is even more true since the proletariat is not a single subject at all but an aggregate of separate individuals, wage-laborers, who have the potential for becoming a collective. Militants are therefore faced not with a single dependent person but with a whole class of dependent persons (wage-slaves),[15] with opportunities for advocating emancipation (maturity) correspondingly changed, shifted, limited. Vanguardists try to force the revolution. Real proletarian revolutionaries recognize that any attempt to do so is folly, a retrogression. This is a major difference between Marx on the one hand and Lassalle (the totalitarian patronizer) on the other, one of Marx's main opponents within the nineteenth century movement. Vanguardists patronize and matronize the proletariat. They delude themselves that they can do something which in fact proletarians can only do

15 A slave is, by definition, a dependent person. Thus no matter how self-reliant and independent any individual wage-slave may seem to be that laborer is still dependent, by virtue of their objective position.

for themselves. This is the difference that split Lenin and Martov. Lenin felt that emancipation could be brought to the proletariat from the outside. Martov realized that it could only be achieved from the inside. They built their respective strategies accordingly. Lenin's program prevailed. But it had nothing to do with proletarian emancipation any more than an over-protective mother's `help' and `love' for her dependent child ever leads to the child's maturity.

I do not mean to assert here that a person's growth toward maturity is in any sense a natural process, any more than the proletariat's movement toward self-emancipation is an inevitable development. Proletarians need never and may never escape wage-slavery and achieve freedom. There are good reasons to hope that they will but it is in no sense inevitable. This is so because humans make their own history, even if under conditions not of their own choosing. If freedom were inevitable it wouldn't be freedom, would it? Similarly, a person need not reach maturity. Millions of people in the capitalist societies never do, perhaps even the majority. (In any case, real maturity is impossible for a wage-slave and constitutes rather a main objective of the revolution.) Maturity can be achieved only under certain conditions. But it is in no sense determined by those conditions because maturity is also a question of a person's response to external conditions. Nor does this make maturity indeterminate. Determinate/indeterminate is another one of those bourgeois dualities. The two elements — the external conditions and a person's response to those conditions — cannot be separated. Some individuals achieve maturity under conditions that stymie most people while others fail to under conditions that usually nurture.

This line of reasoning helps to unravel one of the more puzzling (and painful) paradoxes of the struggle for emancipation — the seemingly greater power of the organizers. The Marxists-Leninists never tire of reminding us that we cannot hope to defeat the bourgeoisie without organization, and anyone who opposes organization is branded an anarchist. The trouble with this, as I have argued above, is that it treats organization in a false, abstract way, not distinguishing hierarchical organization from democratic organization. Thus they see only two options — fanatic individualism or organization. Their strategy seeks to build a hierarchical force comparable in every way to that of the bourgeoisie except stronger. They seek to outdo the bourgeoisie at its own game. I do not believe that the bourgeoisie can be defeated in this way, but unfortunately, the superior strength of egalitarian organization is rarely recognized. This is one of the things that stymies the proletarian revolution, and the vanguardists deserve a lot of the blame for this situation.

There is no denying that hierarchical organization is a formidable power. It's relative puniness will be demonstrated only when, and if, a genuinely democratic revolutionary movement gets under way. If the proletarian revolution ever gets off the ground the might of the bourgeoisie will crumble like tinsel. Nevertheless, hierarchy is a powerful force when opposed only by atomized and passive masses.

Getting the revolution underway depends on consciousness, intent, and clarity of goals. It has to be *desired* by the majority of wage-slaves. The desire and vision is what is missing. If that existed it would be a different story. Until it does exist, until the commitment to democracy and egalitarian relations gathers steam, hierarchy is a formidable weapon for anyone willing to use it, for the bourgeoisie for example in relation to the proletariat, as well as for sectarian groups in relation to other radicals and other sectarian groups.

Let me now consider this paradox (of the seemingly greater power of the organizers) at the level of the small group. Suppose for example that a group of people is engaged in a discussion and debate about what kind of politics to adopt. Suppose further that there are three main politics being advanced for consideration in the group by at least one spokesperson each, but that the majority of people in the group remain undecided, listening to the arguments, trying to make up their minds. One political tendency is individualism (egoism) (liberalism, pluralism, love and harmony, do-your-own-thing'ism, smooth-over-the-differences). Another is vanguardism (hierarchy, authoritarianism, dogmatism, solidarity, discipline, let's-all-do-it-together-my-way'ism). A third tendency is communism (egalitarianism, democracy, collectivity, majority rule, four way criticism).

If most people opt ultimately for the individualist position it is difficult to see how the group can thereafter have any common policies or programs at all since the prior agreement, their basis of unity so to speak, their only common bond, is that people will do their own thing, which precludes, by definition, common programs. In the second and third tendencies however common programs are possible. If those in the group fighting for the democratic regime fail to win over the majority of the group and instead find that the majority comes down in favor of hierarchy, authoritarianism, and discipline, subsequently dividing themselves into leaders and followers, the democrats are stymied in their effort to win an egalitarian regime, certainly as long as the majority does not adopt democracy as its own program.

It is common to think that this situation (of being dependent upon majority support) does not apply in the case of the vanguardists who, it is thought, can impose an authoritarian regime against majority will, thus giving them an advantage over the egalitarians, whose program depends upon majority support before it can be effected. When examined in the context of the small group it is clear that this is not so. To think thus is to neglect the problem of passivity. The vanguardists depend every bit as much upon majority support as do the democrats. Leaders cannot exist without followers.

The defeat of egalitarian politics is therefore due as much to the followers as it is to the leaders. That is, it is due as much to passivity as it is to domination, perhaps more so. We have all experienced what happens to an influential person in a group when others stop listening to and agreeing with that person, and instead turn their backs on him or her, withdrawing their support. The leader is no longer the leader. Leaders have no more power than is given them by those who follow. This is a commonplace. Unfortunately its real import is not often grasped. Instead, the vanguard's call for organization continues to seem relevant, whereas actually it misses the point completely. The point is this: that while domination and passivity go hand in hand, in terms of achieving emancipation passivity is the greater obstacle, the prior element. Of course tanks and machine guns do exist (as do administrative controls), and they have considerable power to impose themselves (if deployed by real live persons) regardless of the consciousness of those they are directed against. Even if proletarians were radical therefore they would still have to face the military and administrative might of the bourgeoisie.

But this is my point. The might of the bourgeoisie and hence its capacity to impose an authoritarian regime against the will of the proletariat is a short-run capacity. There can be no doubt whatsoever that proletarians could eventually succeed in overthrowing the bourgeoisie if they ever set their minds to the task. The problem is they have never set their minds to the task. They have remained passive with regard to the goal of abolishing wage-slavery. The vanguard, in spite of its organizing to build up the mass base, does not really even perceive passivity as a key problem and does not focus proper attention on it.

On the contrary, far from seeking to bring into being an active proletariat, vanguardists want a disciplined proletariat. Thus instead of opposing passivity they foster it. A disciplined person, a person who does what he's told without asking questions, is a passive person. Vanguardists therefore depend on a passive proletariat just like the ruling class does. The leaders are active but the workers are passive, vis-à-vis the leaders, however actively they might fight for the vanguard victory. The stress in the vanguard strategy is just the opposite of what it should be. The focus is on the wrong half of the duality – on domination, on overthrowing the ruling class – rather than on the prior element, passivity. That is, organizers seek to end domination (by building the vanguard party) with never any thought of putting an end to passivity. Actually, what they are really attempting to do is end domination by *building* passivity (discipline).

Nothing shows the utter bankruptcy of vanguard politics better than this. It is clear that it is only their own passivity they are attempting to end, and this by exploiting the passivity of the masses. Thus the whole question of consciousness is simply not a meaningful topic for vanguardists, in spite of the volumes they have written about false consciousness. They think the problem is one of organization.[16]

It should go without saying that the ruling class is not going to stop dominating; therefore working class will have to stop *being* dominat-

---

16 False Consciousness, like all vanguard concepts, is formulated from an outside point of view. It presupposes the possibility of a true consciousness, or a correct one as Marxists-Leninists are fond of saying. It is thus merely one more manifestation of the fallacy of objectivism. What exists in reality is not true and false consciousness, but agreement and disagreement. Moreover it is in large measure because most people in the core capitalist countries perceive these societies as democratic (not as totalitarian) and see themselves as citizens (not as slaves) that these societies continue to exist as they do. It is this perception, widely shared and agreed upon, that holds things together in the last analysis, not physical force. If most people ever came to perceive themselves as slaves this would itself be a mighty force. Thus this so-called false consciousness does not merely reflect, it creates, reality; it is real,

ed. It must end its passivity. This feat is within its power. Only then could the other half of the problem, domination, be faced effectively. It is of course through the process of opposing domination that one overcomes passivity. Nevertheless there is an important difference of stress depending upon which element is seen as prior.

Consider this so-called greater power of the organizers now in the context of the revolutionary movement in general and on the national level. Exactly the same thing holds as holds in the small group. If I am Martov and have spent my whole life agitating for the self-emancipation of the proletariat but nobody listens, and if instead the overwhelming majority rallies behind Lenin, who calls for hierarchy and discipline in order to bring emancipation to the proletariat from the outside, this says nothing except that nobody listened (leaving aside questions of tactical error or failure of will in fighting to get the majority to adopt the democratic tendency as its own). It does not say that my program wouldn't have worked or that my strategy wouldn't have brought down the bourgeoisie if it had been adopted and tried. We could talk of a failure of the strategy only if it had been adopted and pursued as vigorously as the vanguard strategy was. It is not a failure when something does not happen if

just as the commodity, fetish though it is, is also *the real thing.*

90

it has not even been sought. Yet the fact that Lenin won is used as evidence that his strategy was correct. What nonsense. What really happened is that most proletarians, for whatever reasons, never even embraced (at least during the crucial months leading up to the Bolshevik take-over) the real goal (democratic collectivity), and instead opted for a rather different goal (the tightly disciplined vanguard party's seizure of power).

If the sectarians in the movement band themselves together into hierarchical organizations whereas the genuine revolutionaries remain fragmented, atomized, and isolated, it is no wonder that the vanguardists (and organization) seem to have an edge over egalitarian politics. Organizations (either hierarchical or democratic) can accumulate greater resources than can individuals working alone and can maintain a historical presence transcending the life of any given member. They can raise money to support full-time militants, start publishing houses, make films, print newspapers, organize legal defenses, collect bail funds, and so forth. Egalitarian militants need not remain fragmented, however. Historically I think they have, for whatever reason, perhaps because third road radicals have been so few in number, but perhaps also because they have sometimes confused fighting with elitism itself. This is a very serious error. There is no reason why genuine communists can't get themselves together to agitate for their politics just like the vanguardists and other bogus radicals do. To fail to do so in fact is to hand over the revolution to the vanguardists on a silver platter (and hence to the counter-revolution). Nobody is going to give us freedom. To fail to fight for it is only to acquiesce in being trampled into the dirt by the organizers.

I think there has been a further, very serious, confusion in the stance of third tendency revolutionaries toward vanguardists: the failure to distinguish between the organization of subsocietal groupings (be they hierarchical or democratic) and the organization of the entire society. Hierarchy (like violence), as evil as it is, might conceivably be tolerated as a means which might contribute, under certain circumstances, to reaching the goal of communism (the nonhierarchical society), just as violence might conceivably be used to bring into being a nonviolent society. Thus it is conceivable that a group of people organized hierarchically could agitate for the self-emancipation of the proletariat. Obviously however, in order not to confuse this with vanguarding, they would have to distinguish clearly between their own organization (as protagonists) and the proletariat's future organization (created for the purposes of its self-government) and would therefore have to refrain from seizing power themselves, even if faced with the opportunity to do so.

This is why Marx ridiculed Bakunin's idea

that the IWA was the embryo of the future proletarian society. For Marx the IWA was a special purpose organization whose functions were quite limited. It was not the embryo of anything. It was designed merely to agitate and educate, and to advance the proletarian point of view. Although there is no good reason, generally speaking, why the organizations militants create can't be democratic, there may be occasions when a hierarchical organization makes good sense.

Vanguardists do not make these distinctions, however, and thus confuse the party's seizure of power with the proletariat's seizure of power. They plan to extend the hierarchical organization of their own voluntary association (the Party) to the society as a whole upon victory. That is, the Party, which is hierarchical, simply becomes the Government. This is why they must be opposed as counter-revolutionary and defeated, and not merely because they adopt a hierarchical form internally in their own organization.

This argument has important implications for the question of national organizations in the radical movement. For a number of years I opposed all national organizations of radicals because I felt they were inevitably hierarchical. This was a mistake, as the arguments above show. It is not the hierarchy of an organization or its national character that makes it vanguard, but its goal, its conception of the revolution as the installation of a so-called socialist government in Washington.

Nevertheless, there was a second error in my opposition to national organizations which tends to shift the argument back the other way, against hierarchy. I felt then that national organizations were inevitably hierarchical because it seemed to me impossible under present conditions to base decision-making in such an organization on direct democracy. Even in the best of cases I felt that national organizations could only be built on the basis of representative democracy, which is a bourgeois form of organization. I no longer believe this is true. I doubt if any national voluntary association has ever been based on direct democracy so far but I think one very well might be, and the effort to do so would be good training for the proletarian revolution.

None of these complexities seem to get in the way of the Marxists-Leninists. It is no wonder then that their vision of the revolution prevails, and has for decades, being challenged only by periodic upsurges of liberal reformism. Proletarian revolutionaries are hardly even in the arena yet. It is vanguardism that is in the air, creating the stench.

I suspect there is an element of temperament involved as well in this seemingly greater power of the organizers. Many people hate being on bottom because they are not on top rather than because there is a top and a bottom to begin with. Thus they oppose domination only because they want to install themselves in power. To be a proletarian however I have to be disposed simultaneously to resist being dominated and to refrain from dominating. I have to oppose the oppressor without becoming an oppressor myself. If I am a middle child, for example, and I hate the domination of my Big Brother or Sister, I must refuse to be a Big Brother or Sister to my younger sibling if I want to be consistent in my hatred of domination.

This requires a peculiar and I think rare (at least so far) temperament. Capitalism tends to reproduce the domination/passivity syndrome, with most people usually exhibiting more of one trait than the other. Even so, both horns of the duality always come together as a pair, as a package deal. The tough guy for instance always has an idol somewhere to whom he defers. I was struck while watching Ehrlichman during the Watergate hearings, one of Nixon's meanest lieutenants, by how he had apparently taken over many of Nixon's mannerisms, expressions, and gestures. At the same time though it was clear that he dished it out to others the same way Nixon dished it out to him. He accepted discipline from Nixon and expected others to accept it from him. Passive toward the superior but dominant toward the subordinate.

In recent years I have come to view this pattern as exceedingly strange, weird, freakish almost, even pathological. It seems to me almost schizophrenic. Ehrlichman emulated Nixon but patronized everyone else. A proletarian revolutionary is passive toward no one and dominant toward no one, but rather simultaneously opposes both tendencies, neither emulating nor tutoring. This is a difficult stance to take, and, if not taken properly and firmly, can land you on your ass, if, for example, you not only refuse to dominate but also refuse to fight to impose proletarian democracy on all the elitists, vanguardists, leaders, bullies, patrons, rulers, organizers, oppressors, manipulators, aggressors, bosses, Priests, Capitalists, and Mothers who oppose it, as well as upon all the individualists, neutralists, abstainers, pacifists, withdrawers, pluralists, tolerators, followers, and spoiled brats.

Only a majority of the society can succeed in imposing such a regime, and only from their position as wage-slaves. But this is not domination. It is the overthrow of domination. There will obviously be coercion even under proletarian democracy – the domination of the majority over the minority. All societies are coercive in the sense that nowhere are individuals autonomous. Humans are social animals. The fight then is over whether a minority will rule or the majority. Commitment to majority rule means that I have to be an egalitarian, and a person with collective sentiments. I have to think for myself but yet not be an individualist. I have to be willing to go along with the majority but yet refuse to take orders from any autocrat. It seems to me that the genuinely proletarian temperament has only a very precarious foothold in a few of the core capitalist societies. It leads a very uncertain existence. It's like a threatened species. There is absolutely no guarantee that it will survive since the forces arrayed against it are staggering.

There is one main point yet to be made about the seemingly greater power of the organizers. Marxists-Leninists believe that only a strong, hierarchical, tightly disciplined party can defeat the bourgeoisie. It seems to me that this is about the shoddiest and clumsiest misjudgment in the whole Book of Vanguard Errors. No matter how disruptive the masses get, the very idea that a centralized voluntary organization with a Central Committee and Leaders can topple the concentrated power of a government in a modern capitalist state is so far out it hardly even deserves consideration. It is absurd on the face of it. Granting the idea all the credit one can muster for it, such an event can be imagined as happening only under the rarest of circumstances. The bourgeoisie would have to be in complete and utter disarray, and the society in mortal chaos for a party to be able to seize the state.

It is unlikely that such a situation will

ever arise under organized capitalism, notwithstanding periodic crises. And if it did arise, if mortal chaos did develop, it is a certainty that it would be the fascists who would step in to restore order, not the Left. And if it were the Left, and not the Right, which stepped in, what would that show? Isn't that only another indication that the Old Left has dictatorial ambitions? Is there a democratic way out of chaos? Would democracy be a possibility at that point? Much of the strategic thinking of the Old Left has been built upon a crisis theory of one kind or another, the projected inevitable collapse of capitalism. The Party, while not necessarily waiting for such a crisis, nevertheless must be prepared to exploit it when it does come. Exploiting the crisis means installing itself in power by exploiting peoples' dire need for things to continue to hang together enough to ensure physical survival. In the United States there is no chance whatsoever that a communist party could take over the state during a chaotic breakdown of the system. It will never happen. It will be a right-winger, someone like Goldwater or Reagan, some champion of the Common People, not the CP. And if it were the CP it would amount to the same thing, dictatorship.

The overwhelming weight of evidence speaks against the feasibility of a vanguard party's seizure of power in any Western capitalist country, crisis or no crisis. Governments in these societies have expanded in size a thousand fold over their nineteenth century predecessors. They employ up to fifteen percent of the entire labor force. They have vast secret police establishments and enormous intelligence and surveillance capabilities. They have the resources to assign a hundred agents if they so desire to observe and infiltrate any subversive group that might raise its head. Police in these countries have at their disposal a vast array of armaments: centralized and computerized data banks, tanks, mace, gas, helicopters, radio communications, pellet rifles, and so forth, plus the usual arsenal of machine guns, grenades, pistols, rifles, and shotguns. In addition, the technology of nonlethal force is now beginning to emerge and is perhaps the most formidable weapon yet to appear.

Moreover, there is no possibility that the government won't be able to recruit enough personnel for these armies of guards, police, and spies. Even if the vast majority of the population were hostile to the government the state would still be able to find its quota of fascist SS types to staff a professional military force strong enough to quell any disorderly uprising. (It is only an orderly uprising that they would not be able to quell.) Can you even imagine a Red Army trooping back and forth across the United States in a Long March, or the establishment of Red Bases in the Rockies, or anywhere else. It's pure fantasy. There is no question in my mind that the core capitalist states now have and will continue to have the capacity to smash to smithereens any voluntary association within its boundaries if it so chooses. There is moreover not the slightest doubt that it *will* so choose if such an organization begins to look the least bit threatening. The fate of the Black Panthers is a case in point.

I have presented this argument before, only to receive in reply the claim that all this is only that much more reason to pick up the fight and take on the state/army/police. In other words, it was seen as a question of courage. The fact that they can blow any vanguard party to kingdom come is not perceived as tactically significant, calling for caution, or a revision of strategy. Rather, it is seen as a challenge, all the more reason, it is said, to organize the New Communist Party and get on with the revolution against bourgeois power. It is always assumed of course that a party is an inevitable aspect of such an undertaking. This is a foolish stance. There is nothing courageous about offering oneself up for slaughter. That is only stupid. Courage is when I risk my neck for the chance that I might win, knowing also that I might lose. There is no risk involved in the vanguard party strategy because defeat is a virtual certainty. Victory is a possibility only as a freak event. To fight for the vanguard party's seizure of power therefore is not a courageous thing, it is merely dumb. The claim that organizers have more power against the bourgeoisie than do egalitarian militants is thus a myth. It is a wonder that the idea continues to have any credibility at all since in the West the party has never been able to do what it says it is going to do. Seventy-five dreary years of failure do not prove that a strategy is wrong, but it is cause enough to make you ponder the question. Marxists-Leninists apparently are too obtuse to ponder such a doubt.

The Marxist-Leninist belief that the tightly disciplined party can seize power and lead the proletariat to freedom is matched for sheer nonsense only by the individualist illusion that freedom can be won by withdrawing from the political arena altogether. One can sympathize a little with the Marxists-Leninists when confronted by the truly massive and exasperating upsurge of individualism that appeared in the New Left in the late sixties and early seventies as thousands of radicals retired to rural communes to groove on personal relations inside their own little groups. This was always done in the name of collectivity of course, but it was a collectivity so truncated as to lose all political significance. The retreat to communes actually marked the abandonment of any comprehension of the society as a whole and exposed a willingness to seek salvation within the established order. Do-your-own-thing'ism is possible only within the larger framework of a hierarchical society and within the limits established by that society. It is a tendency that is especially congenial to capitalism, perhaps even limited to capitalism. Individualism represents a capitulation to the atomizing force of the bourgeois world, not its transcendence. The Marxists-Leninists must themselves be held partially responsible for this since it is not difficult to see why so many thousands of militants turn their backs on the nauseating dogmatism that flows incessantly and aggressively out of the dozens of would-be Parties.

The really awful thing about the New Left of the sixties is that it failed so completely, after all that commotion, to transcend the limits of the Old Left and break out into a new political vision. For those with no clear picture of the democratic alternative, there was nothing else to do, if they also refused to become obnoxious, proselytizing vanguards, except withdraw again into private life. There was nowhere else to go politically, given the collapse of the New Left. If you are trapped inside the duality there are only two options – egoism and vanguardism, New Left do-your-own-thing'ism and Old Left do-it-our-way-or-else'ism. The selection of the individualist option at least leaves you on the side of the domina*ted* rather than the domina*tors*. If it is impossible to be free, it is usually the superior choice (if you have a choice) to be the slave rather than the master. That puts you in the right position at least, with the whole world as your future. But if you are the master you are trapped, unable to move forward to freedom, unless, that is, you desert and join the slaves. If it is in such instances better to be dominated than to dominate, it is also, on the other hand, better to win than to lose. Winning and dominating are not synonymous. In fact, dominating represents defeat not victory. Vanguardists are unable to make this distinction. Dominating and winning are synonymous in their book because winning means the imposition of, not the will of the majority, but the will of the radicals, the party, or the Central Committee.

If it is impossible to make the revolution *for* the proletariat (or to win freedom by withdrawing from the struggle for power altogether), this does not mean that protagonists of the proletariat should sit on their hands and wait for some magical proletarian uprising. They can agitate. To wait, twiddling one's thumbs, is to fall into the trap of spontaneism. As a rule, whenever anyone opposes the vanguard's attempt to bring the revolution to the proletariat from the outside this is the accusation that is always forthcoming – spontaneism. Actually however, spontaneism and vanguardism are but opposite sides of the same coin, twin horns of the same duality. Those impaled on one of the horns tend to perceive only the other horn. That's why vanguardists always perceive their democratic opponents as individualists (or anarchists in their warped terminology).

Spontaneism was a pronounced tendency in the revisionist (liberal) wing of the Second International. A hybrid version of the species is also quite pronounced in our own time, but in unsuspected fields. It can be found thriving mainly among the very same groups who so constantly rail against it. Today, spontaneism sneaks into the movement in the guise of Third Worldism. Third Worldism is a deeply entrenched outlook across most sections of the Old Left in the U.S., as well as throughout most of the New Left. Third Worldists hang their hats on some one or another of the so-called communist revolutions in the colonies and neo-colonies, with splits occurring over which revolution the hat is hung on. Third Worldists see the enemy as imperialism rather than capitalism. The Monthly Review Press over the years since World War II is a good example of this tendency in the Old Left. Most of its books have focused on revolutions in the Third World, although there has been a very slight shift to a domestic or Western European focus in recent years. The majority of its publications however are still Third World. The Weatherman underground is a good example of the tendency in the New Left. These groups put an overwhelming stress on

Third World Revolutions. They do not seem to believe that a revolution is even on the agenda in the core capitalist countries and do not seek to build toward that end. It is almost as if they expect the revolution to be brought to the U.S. from the outside by the victorious Communist Parties of the Third World, which will slowly chip away at the Empire until it either collapses of its own weight, can be easily taken from the outside, or is cut down in size enough so that an indigenous working class can do the job itself. The working class in such schemes is either not even recognized, or if it is, it is perceived as hostile to the revolution (the New Left), or else it is patronized something terrible and is seen as something to be brought around to the revolution through manipulation (the Old Left).

In any case, the upshot of all this is that for Third Worldists the revolution in our own country is neglected, postponed, or avoided. More effort is put into supporting revolution elsewhere than into building toward revolution at home. Needless to say, this is not what I mean by agitating.

It is important to distinguish at this point between agitating (being a protagonist) and the Politics of Support. I have always been against the politics of support, from its earliest appearance in the movement. I perceived it as a condescending stance, which it is, and have argued instead that revolutionaries must fight their own oppression, not support someone else's fight against oppression. By the summer of 1970 I had even moved to oppose the anti-war movement, arguing that it was getting to be a major obstacle in the way of building toward revolution, saying that a strategy to end the war in Vietnam and a strategy to make the revolution here were not necessarily the same things and were probably even in conflict. It might seem at first glance that my protagonist is merely engaged in a politics of support. This is not so, and I want to try to show why.

Let me consider the Old Left version of this, leaving aside the New Left version, as it appeared, say, in the late SDS, where the youth movement was seen as a support movement for Third World revolutions, whose function was to harass the empire from inside the bowels of the monster. The dominant sects in the Old Left are riddled with a support politics orientation. This support, naturally, is given from the point of view of The Welders. Vanguard Parties like SWP put stress on blacks, women, Puerto Ricans, Chicanos, and Indians because they see these as ``the most oppressed peoples.'' It is the structuralist thing. These groups are the parts of the structure that are in revolt. It is only by welding all these revolting peoples into a solid block that the revolution can be achieved.

Thus a politics of support is an incredibly manipulative, condescending, patronizing politics. The supporters are using these groups to further their own end, which is to build a mass base for the party's seizure of power. They see these oppressed peoples as detonating larger and larger revolts, revolts which will at some point bring the working class itself into the movement. The role, usually unstated, of the party in all this is central and, once seen, shows that the support offered in these cases is not because of an interest in the self-emancipation of those exploited peoples, but flows instead out of an interest in bringing revolution to them from above through the hoped for victory of the party.

The relationship of the vanguard to these groups cannot be understood separately from the vanguard's overall conception of the revolution and how to make it. One of the most repulsive experiences you can have is to go to a mass rally organized by the SWP and never once hear the words revolution or socialism (let alone communism) spoken in a whole afternoon of speeches. This is because these vanguardists are speaking ``on the level of the people.'' They refrain from talking straight and laying their cards on the table because they don't want to alienate the workers, who are not thought to be ready yet for any talk about revolution. It is only in stages, as their consciousness improves, that radical notions like revolution can be fed to the workers. This is one of the main reasons for mass rallies in the first place. It is felt that if you can get people to come to a mass rally and listen to liberal speeches this will pull them into the movement, get them involved, and start them down the long road of radicalization, under the careful tutelage of the party of course. I have always detested being talked down to, and that's what a politics of support amounts to. It is gross manipulation pure and simple. It has nothing to do with agitation for the self-emancipation of proletarians.

I got a big dose of being talked down to as a young man and I had an instinctively hostile reaction to it. There was a professor at the junior college I attended, one of the dominant figures on campus, who took this stance toward his students and also, since he was a minister and professor of theology, toward the campus congregation. In class he openly advocated beginning ``on the level of the people.'' That was one of the rules for effective ministry and teaching. His theology also incorporated this notion. God always worked on the level of the people, he argued. That is why you can see an evolution in conceptions of divinity, for example, because God only gives humankind as much knowledge as it can absorb at any one time. I even wrote a paper on the evolution of the idea of the Kingdom in the Old Testament, reflecting these views.

But on another level I was always uneasy with this stance of his. In my sophomore year I began to get increasingly frustrated with it. I wanted to know what he really believed. I felt that I was ready to hear the whole story, the best that he could deliver. I wanted to judge for myself whether I believed it or not. I pressed him several times in class to lay it out, to tell us his real beliefs, but to no avail. He held back, or at least he gave that impression, or made that pretense. I eventually concluded that he didn't have anything more to say and that we had heard it all, even though he always gave the impression of only giving us as much as he thought we could absorb. But to this day I have never learned whether or not this was true or whether he was really holding back. (Late in life he became a Patriarch in the Church.) My friends and I reacted by adopting as our stance that bitterly cynical religious humor (which becomes hypocritical if adopted as a permanent outlook and style) which so characterizes, even now, anti-authoritarian circles inside the Church.

A protagonist's agitation for the self-emancipation of proletarians is straightforward and on the level. It is precisely this recognition that they (the protagonists) *cannot* make the revolution themselves, and the refusal to even try to, that enables protagonists to relate to proletarians in an egalitarian rather than a patronizing way. There is no way that they can use the proletariat for their own ends since they have adopted as their own goal the (implicit) goal of proletarians themselves – collective self-emancipation and collective self-government. Even if this goal is for now only imputed to the proletariat by the protagonists of the proletariat its very nature prohibits manipulation on the part of those agitating for revolution. When I am a protagonist of the proletariat I am inside the revolution even if I am not inside a factory or office and hence I am on a level with and equal to proletarians. I relate to them on the basis of egalitarian reciprocity, not on the basis of deference or tutelage. This is not a politics of support. It is agitation for a proletarian revolution. Obviously, only proletarians can make it. It is a question of getting the revolution into the air. If as many people were engaged in agitating for a Third Road politics as are now involved in the catastrophes of the Old Left and the New Left then maybe things would begin to move. Many of the activities these people would do would ostensibly be the same activities that now occupy Old Left and New Left radicals. They would occupy buildings, make films, give speeches, put out newspapers, protest, talk to workers, publish books, demonstrate, do research, hand out leaflets, confront the bourgeoisie, resist oppression, and so forth. But the content, the goal, and hence the politics of these so-called activities would be very different than, and contrary to, vanguardism and individualism.

[17]{The problem we are dealing with here, if

17 The entire following discussion of radicalization,

110

we begin with the premise that the revolution must be made by the proletarian majority itself, is the problem of the radicalization of the working class, the question of winning over the majority. This is a vast and complex topic, intimidating in its scope, and all I can do here is wade in and hope I don't drown. I used to believe that radicalization would grow only as (a) more and more radicals agitated constantly and in every way possible for the proletarian revolution, and (b) as more and more radicals began to struggle directly to establish a network of councils and direct democracy, if they were in a position to do so. I still believe this but it can't be left at this because it doesn't say a great deal about the process of radicalization or how to bring it about, problems that are nicely buried in the innocent looking phrase `more and more'.

Recently, moreover, I have come to

which I have placed in brackets, was written from an outside stance, since it assumes throughout that there exists an objective definition of radical, even though I rejected this position earlier in the paper, and even though in these passages themselves I hammer away at objectivism in round about ways. I only noticed what had happened after rereading it. I have decided to let the passages stand as is however as a warning and as an example of what the problem is and of the insidious grip that vanguard tendencies have. The task, after all, is not to convert someone or everyone, but to create a situation where everyone gets to vote. The notion of winning over implies an outside stance. If the majority were in fact in power, with everyone having a say in policy deliberations, who would there be to say that any given decision wasn't radical?

have my doubts even about the very image of radicalization that is standard in the movement, namely that radicalization is something that will happen as a result of the efforts of militants. The efforts of militants will be (or could be) an important element in this, but only indirectly in a sense, and the relationship between these efforts and any possible radicalization of the majority is very poorly understood. There is of course a possible relationship between a minority outlook and any shift in the majority outlook (between for example the beliefs of anti-war demonstrators and a subsequent shift in majority opinion about the war, like occurred in the late sixties in the United States), but this is a complex relationship, certainly not a simple, direct one. The minority view does not necessarily directly cause the change in the majority view, even if it has an impact. In fact, in the example cited, you might even argue that the majority in the U.S. came to oppose the war in Vietnam *in spite of* the efforts of radicals, since notwithstanding its opposition to the war the majority remains deeply hostile to the radical movement. That is, radicalization is something that might more plausibly be viewed as a development *internal* to the majority world outlook, or so it will seem. Thus perhaps radicalization will be based on and grow out of the popular, predominant, mass consciousness and majority outlook. Perhaps it will be a change *within* popular consciousness as a response to the logic of events themselves. It might even happen through the mass media and in spite of the intended message of the media. Millions of people will get the point, acquire a knowledge of the reality behind the appearances, and come to an understanding of what is really going on in spite of the objective content of what is told them. This is a possibility at least.

Moreover, it could happen fairly quickly, even overnight perhaps. A majority conviction that the U.S. is not a democracy for example (contrary to previous beliefs) could emerge rapidly given a certain sequence of events. Many radicals, especially vanguardists, too often fail to take into account the prevailing world outlook and its internal structure and dynamics. Or rather they have an uninformed, incorrect conception of this. They tend to see other people's ideas and beliefs like they do their own, as objects that can be lifted bodily out of a person, through proselytizing, and replaced by a new set. They seem to think that radical ideas can be brought to people from the outside, failing to notice the internal aspects of anyone's becoming a radical. Hence they fail to understand properly the relationship between people who are radical and people who are not radical. I doubt very much (on one level) that radicalization is a question of winning over more and more people to radical views until finally radicals outnumber the nonradicals, half plus one. Rather, the shift from a bourgeois framework into the proletarian framework might conceivably happen relatively quickly, and on a massive scale, although the winning over process might be going on in the background as well.

I can just hear someone saying right now that this argument shows that I am a spontaneist after all in spite of my earlier disclaimers. I want to point out therefore that I have nowhere said that radicals should sit on their hands and wait for this to happen. Nor have I said that there is *no* connection between the efforts of militants and the radicalization process. What I have said is that the image that many radicals have of winning over people, one by one, to the revolution is probably a faulty conceptualization of the radicalization process and therefore leads to faulty tactics. Tactics might be more justifiably designed to recognize this other process, fit into it, be based on it. There is moreover the additional complication that there is absolutely no guarantee that such an enlightenment will ever happen, and it is thus certainly not predictable. The radical viewpoint already exists in our society and has for decades, or at least some rather pathetic versions of it have. Yet it confronts the majority as an outside, minority viewpoint, on the fringe of society. Nor is this due entirely to successful bourgeois efforts to portray it as such, but stems also, it seems to me, from tactics radicals themselves have used.

Nevertheless, this is tricky question. What tactics could possibly avoid such a phenomenon (of being perceived as an outside, minority faction)? Revolution is after all a minority viewpoint at present and also one that is hostile to the current viewpoint of the majority, although not to the majority itself (according to radicals). I would never argue for example that radicals should never offend majority sentiments. That would put us in a position of talking down to and patronizing nonradicals. Far better to play it straight. If the Vietcong flag is a worthy symbol, fly it. If words like capitalism and imperialism and petty bourgeois are good solid concepts, use them, even though they turn people off. The idea that you can't do this or that for fear of turning people off puts you squarely in the manipulator's camp. It means you are protecting other people and not treating them like adults who can decide for themselves whether to agree or disagree with your views. It is, moreover, sneaky. It is backhanded. It lacks candor. It is dishonest and conniving. It is also weak, since it accepts the ban that has been imposed on these words and deeds by the bourgeoisie. To accept such a ban, even tactically in hopes of winning over workers by speaking on their level, plays right into the hands of the ruling class. The struggle is as much to be able to say authentic proletarian words, or even to think them, amidst the smothering mendacity of bourgeois culture, as it is anything. When radicals say they are afraid of turning people off it is probably safe to infer that they are also afraid of turning people on. (The very phrases are elitist, since they imply controlling or manipulating people like objects.) This is certainly true for outfits like SWP whose whole program it sometimes seems could only have been designed with one aim in mind: to avoid revolution. This is not to question the genuineness of their commitment, but only the wisdom of their strategy.

None of this has anything to do with spontane*ism* however even though there is undeniably an element of spontaneity at work, in the sense that it is impossible to know before it happens whether or not any given proletarian (or the majority of proletarians) will become radical. You certainly can't predict it. It depends upon a worker's response to the situation. Just as you cannot say, until it happens, that a child will achieve maturity, so also with the radicalization of a proletarian. A person may remain a child their whole life long. A slave may never adopt the consciousness of being a slave. A wage-laborer may never become radical.[18] To this extent then there is an

18 I am not saying that proletarians are like children. On the contrary, I am trying to expose the condescension in the strategy of the vanguardists which results from their failure to recognize that radicalization cannot be forced from the outside. If it could be they would have done it long ago. But fortunately it is not something over which they exercise any control.

element of spontaneity involved. If there were no spontaneity involved in becoming a radical how could it have anything at all to do with freedom. Even though there are many things radicals can do to create conditions conducive to radicalization there is nothing anyone can actually do to impose a radical consciousness on workers. Workers either get a radical consciousness, by themselves ultimately, or they don't get it at all. In this sense therefore the hands of radicals *are* tied since they stand helpless, aside from agitation, in front of the continuing passivity (as defined by them) of the working class. As long as slaves do not see themselves as slaves and instead accept their situation as a natural one (or even like being slaves), no matter how onerous it may be, there can never be a revolution. Marx said that ``either the working class is revolutionary or it is nothing.''

One thing at least is fairly certain: outlooks can change overnight almost, or at least very rapidly. The idea then that opinions change only gradually, evolving over long periods of time, is clearly false. The occupation of a factory or office or classroom can literally turn people's heads around. All heads are not turned

If a radical consciousness were something that could be turned on (and off) in others by radicals it wouldn't be worth a dime and would obviously have nothing to do with liberation. It is precisely the recognition that humans are not objects which can be manipulated at will that enables a militant to relate to wage-laborers in an egalitarian way rather than condescendingly.

in the same direction of course. A campus takeover by militants provokes many responses. Looking only at the responses of liberals we see that some join the revolt, others shift right into the fascist camp, while still others stand fast. Nevertheless, a confrontation like that involved in a factory or university occupation can produce very rapid shifts in basic outlooks. This is beyond question.

This adds some weight, it seems to me, to my suspicion that radicalization is not merely a process of winning people over, one by one. Radicalization is one possible response that people can make to *events*, not merely to propaganda. But this is not to say that practice therefore takes priority over theory since the two things can't be separated. Events are not synonymous with action or practice, at least as these latter are dualistically understood. Events involve both actions and ideas. One factory occupation might do more to get the council idea into the air, if successfully articulated that is, than years of propaganda work. It is also possible of course that the bourgeoisie might contain it, or even that it might backfire as did so many of the militant tactics of the New Left, which were perceived by the majority (with a little help from the Establishment) as a threat rather than as a liberating force, and on the same side as they were on.

Radicals need a much more concrete

knowledge of the objective factors that block the radical consciousness from emerging (e.g., the by now intricate internal stratification of the working class, which is by no means entirely accidental), as well as the weapons that are used daily by the bourgeoisie to maintain the hegemony of its world outlook (schools, media, laws, welfare agencies, and so forth). In light of such an understanding it might be possible to devise strategies for countering these forces. Acquiring such a concrete knowledge is part of agitating. To the extent that such knowledge is already on hand for certain individuals and groups it is a question of challenging, exposing, and countering that hegemony wherever possible either individually or in groups. The organizations that are created for these purposes are not particularly problematical. They can be large or small, local or national, democratic or hierarchical, limited in scope or extensive in scope. What is absolutely essential however is that they not set up as a goal their own accession to power. The goal of protagonists, in the organizations they throw up in their nonworking hours, is to undermine three hundred years of bourgeois brainwashing and reduce in every way possible the hegemony of the bourgeoisie, and thus to build toward the proletariat's seizure of power.}

To get beyond these general remarks on agitating it would be necessary to examine more closely specific items of strategy, such as electoral politics, community organizing, unions, guerrilla war, and so forth, and these are issues which I cannot hope to deal with adequately here. Let me round off this discussion for now therefore by considering briefly only one of these: mass demonstrations.

Mass demonstrations have one or two merits, I suppose. They can be (if properly used) but rarely are a means of forcing concessions out of the ruling class. This is about the limit of the tactic's direct effectiveness against bourgeois power. Perhaps more importantly, mass demonstrations can sometimes give a huge moral boost to militants. It shows them they are not alone and gives them courage to continue the struggle. On the positive side of the ledger this is probably their main asset. (But there are very important qualifications even here which I will explain shortly). A militant march side by side with comrades to defy the Establishment can be a real up, a powerful lift for the spirits. No one who has ever participated in such an event (if it is a militant march) can ever forget its effect. The best demonstration I have personally experienced was the march past the Justice Department on November 18, 1969. There were several thousand of us, marching ten to fifteen abreast, with arms locked, chanting, ``Smash the State'' (and also, unfortunately, ``Peace Now''), with Mitchell looking down from his balcony on the top floor. It was powerful.

Of course, in a sense we were merely being tolerated. There were thousands of soldiers deployed inside those huge government buildings and thousands more on alert just a few blocks away. But in another sense we were not at all being tolerated. They didn't want us there but there we were. They had the force to smash us, not we them, but there were also constraints upon their using that force. They would have had to pay a price for the use of blunt force. The professional cops of today know this and avoid it if possible. That's why they're developing nonlethal weapons more and more, even nonlethal bullets. The struggle is always poised I guess on that fine line between what we can get away with and what we pay for with defeat (as long, that is, as the bourgeoisie holds the overwhelming balance of power).

On the other hand, the tremendous lift a person can get from an experience like this is very quickly dissipated. It is ephemeral, almost an illusion. This is not accidental. It follows from the fact that the mass demonstration is itself an ephemeral event, a very temporary thing. The boost that one gets from it dissipates about as fast as the crowd itself dissipates, and people return to their own private, isolated lives.

The main thing wrong with mass demonstrations is thus precisely that they are mass. They do not represent any capacity for genuinely collective action on the part of those involved, but only mass action. This points up why, in the balance, they are more destructive for the revolutionary movement, as presently organized and used, than constructive. The movement continues to take form, in its major confrontations with the bourgeoisie, only as a mass. A mass is inevitably accompanied by leaders – those who call and organize the demonstrations and control also, as a rule, the content of the speeches delivered at the accompanying rallies. In the mass rally, the participants, individual and atomized, return after the rally to their previous state of unrelatedness. Their brief coalescence into a mass is only achieved in fact by their acquiescence in authoritarian patterns, by their willingness to go along with a plan they had no say in developing or deciding upon. All this is because they are suppose to *do* something, and get involved.

We can see the false praxis of the vanguard strategy once again. For most people, for the thousands, for the followers, the practice of the vanguard means for them to pour out into the streets at the designated time and place. Mass rallies continuously function, therefore, whatever other effects they may have upon the ruling class or the individual participants, to strengthen the vanguard groups which organize them. On occasion they even make money for these groups through collections that are taken. They certainly create, almost invariably, a market for selling literature, opportunities for recruitment, and a platform from which to proselytize for vanguard and reformist politics. Hence they are a direct obstacle, in their present form, to building a genuinely revolutionary movement, which must be a movement built on the capacity for collective action, not mass action, and at any time deemed necessary, not only during spring and fall offensives.

If the movement did have an ongoing, permanent capacity to act in a democratic fashion as a collective (that is, consciously, as a result of discussion and majority rule) and not merely through elitist forms, it is conceivable that under these circumstances demonstrations and rallies would be one of the tactics employed. In this case however they would no longer be mass demonstrations. They might be large but not mass, since they would not represent merely a mass of atomized individuals (or groups) but rather an ongoing, functioning collective.

A good case can be made, moreover, that the mass demonstration is a most ineffective tactic. Consider the following: in spite of rare exceptions, a demonstration is basically a form of petitioning the government. The pull of the tactic is in this direction. It is not a tactic designed to deny to the ruling class the power to control our lives. It does not contain within it that potentiality. Rather, it seeks merely to change the minds of the rulers by getting them to change this or that policy. This is certainly important, and can result, if concessions are won, in significant gains for the proletariat. There are even certain political scientists who now incorporate the demonstration into that grab bag of tools (along with the vote, writing one's Congressman) available to citizens in a `democracy' to implement popular sovereignty. They correspondingly advise politicians to view and use demonstrations in this light, so that government might be more `responsive' to the needs of the people. Demonstrations are thus peculiarly dead ended as a struggle for power. They cannot go anywhere or develop, or lead to more powerful forms of militancy.

In fact, the `down' following mass demonstrations is perhaps more notable than the `high' during the event itself, and produces a more powerful and lasting effect on the movement. Moreover, a mass demonstration, if it is a national action (or even a regional action) usually hurts local radical initiatives. It drains the energies and resources of the movement away from alternative strategies, like workplace organizing, for example. Mass demonstrations are furthermore very easily controlled and even manipulated, given gas, crowd infiltrators, and the mass media. Demonstrators are never able to articulate their own rationale for the action to the public at large because these events reach the public mainly through the eyes of the media. A decade of demonstrations did not dent the capacity of the media to convince most people that these were violent actions by minority elements on the fringe of society and thus hostile to the interests of the general population. Demonstrations, finally, serve as a convenient barometer for the police on how strong the resistance is, and even provide them with the opportunity to photograph all the radicals.

We must keep these points in mind when trying to evaluate the boost that we get from attending a march and the fleeting sense of solidarity that it produces. It might be instructive to contrast at this point the lift that I have sometimes had from a march with a very different kind of experience, one that was not merely inspiring but revolutionary. It is one of the few, and without question the most, genuinely revolutionary event that I have experienced to date. It happened at the second annual General Assembly of the Committee of Returned Volunteers. We were midway through the week, and trying to grapple, in a general meeting, with the political implications of various proposed changes in the structure of the organization. This was an exceedingly complex topic. Feelings were running pretty high because the week was slipping away (among other reasons), and we weren't getting much accomplished. Not too far into this particular meeting a rather heated argument broke out between two of the leading men in the organization. This in turn precipitated a women's walkout. All the women in the room got up and left. This was about a year or so after the women's movement began to gather steam in the New Left in the late sixties.

Several hours (and a long women's caucus and a much briefer men's caucus) later the women returned and the meeting reconvened. After a long discussion about sexism the group returned to the topic on the original agenda – structural reforms. Now, however, instead of the discussion being dominated by five or six people, the whole group began to work through the issue. It now became apparent that hardly anybody had understood before what was really going on. Although only one or two men participated in the discussion that ensued, and this marred the event badly, I am convinced that the majority of the men, those who usually sat on the sidelines and did not follow the discussion any more than most of the women, were keenly involved in working through the issue. Slowly, very slowly, those who had formerly not participated in the discussion and had not understood the issue, began to comprehend the problem and move the group toward a policy on the matter.

I think this is one of the most beautiful things I have ever witnessed. I also consider it the most revolutionary thing I have ever witnessed. The sight of formerly passive, uninvolved, intimidated persons rising to an understanding of the issues before them, having put a stop, even if only temporarily, to the aggressive monopolization of decision making by the few, is an experience not to be forgotten soon.

I think the experience was far from perfect, lopsided, and badly marred. I was aware at the time that only one or two men participated in the discussion after the walkout and I didn't like that. I was also aware that four or five women, those who always participated anyway and who consequently understood the issue, carried the burden of the discussion of the structural proposals after the women returned to the meeting. What I oppose is domination and inequality. What so inspired me about the process that unfolded after the walkout was the marked advance that was made toward egalitarianism. It was not until later that the true disaster, in terms of any real advance toward equality, of a split along sex lines (at least as it has unfolded in the last few years) began to sink in. It was not only the leading men who were toppled from influence, but virtually all the men were intimidated into silence. On the other hand, some very powerful and domineering women, in the past allies in every respect to the domineering men in the overall leadership of the organization, were given free reign.

At any rate, for all its defects, this was a revolutionary event because it brought a group of people to a higher level of consciousness and to a greater capacity for self-government than it had possessed before. The group was more of a democratic collective and less of a mass (leaders/followers). This was a very dramatic event therefore but its drama was different than the drama of the march past the Justice Department. I think it was a far more significant drama, of a different order entirely, and the kind that proletarians will experience regularly in their attempts to establish collective self-government through a network of workers councils united on the basis of direct democracy.

www.ingramcontent.com/pod-product-compliance
Lightning Source LLC
Chambersburg PA
CBHW070636030426
42337CB00020B/4037